Radical Christian Living

by

Richard Booker

Destiny Image Publishers
P.O. Box 351
Shippensburg, PA 17257

"Speaking to the Purposes of God for this Generation"

Acknowledgements

My love and gratitude to the following:

My wife, Peggy, for typing the manuscript and for being my first and most important disciple to Jesus.

Those other very special saints of God who have shared their lives with me in a discipling relationship and proven to be faithful in their commitment to Him. Thank you for the blessing of sharing our lives. You will forever be dear and precious to me.

Thanks also to Dr. Paul Yonggi Cho for his kindness to write the foreword and to Danny Carpenter for his fine drawings.

Scriptural quotations have been carefully selected from the following versions of the Bible:

King James Version (KJV)

The New King James Bible, copyright © 1982, Thomas Nelson Inc., Nashville, Tn. (NKJ)

Revised Standard Version, copyright © 1973. (RSV)

Destiny Image Publishers, Inc.®
P.O. Box 351
Shippensburg, PA 17257

First Printing: 1985   Second Printing: 1995

Destiny Image books are available through many distributors outside the United States.

Inside the U.S., call toll free to order:
1-800-722-6774

Contents

About the Author

Richard Booker is an author and Bible teacher presently living in Houston, Texas. His organization, Sounds of the Trumpet, Inc., provides Christian teachings through books, tapes, workshops, etc. Prior to his call to the teaching ministry, Richard was a computer and management consultant, climbing the corporate career ladder. His B.S. and M.B.A. degrees well prepared him. His career became his god, and he spent ten years chasing that elusive idol, dragging his wife, Peggy, across the country with him.

During that time he lectured throughout the United States, Canada and Mexico, training over one thousand management and computer personnel. His more than twenty articles appeared in the leading computer publications. He was listed in *Who's Who in Computers and Automation, Who's Who in Training and Development,* and *The Dictionary of International Biography,* and was a frequent speaker for the American Management Association.

In the middle 1970s, God gave Richard an "Emmaus Road" experience that changed his life. He left his career to devote all his time to writing and teaching about God's Word. He is the author of several books, articles for Christian magazines and other works.

In addition to his Bible classes and teaching tapes, Richard developed and teaches a one-day workshop on how to study the Bible. A list of his Bible study materials is included at the back of this book.

Foreword

"Then said Jesus unto His disciples, 'If any man will come after me, let him deny himself, and take up his cross, and follow me. For whosoever will save his life shall lose it: and whosoever will lose his life for my sake shall find it'."

In the book of Exodus, God changed the bitter water of Marah to sweet water and He is still changing the lives of people who have known the bitterness of sin, disease and the curse. He is giving sweet peace and joy to all who come unto Him because He wants us to live a spiritually and physically healthy and orderly life.

Through my 27 years of ministry I have witnessed countless thousands of such men and women's lives being changed from bitter lives to peaceful and productive lives by receiving Jesus Christ as their Saviour. I can also testify that multitudes of newly born-again as well as luke-warm believers have broken through to a better and nobler living when they decided to follow Jesus' example. Not only were their lives changed but they helped to bring about a change in their families and communities as well, as they fought hard against the prevailing moral decay. We are not machines but we are God's loving children and any social change in our world can only come through an inner revolution within the lives of each of us believers. However, this will happen when we become true disciples of Jesus and not mere believers.

Discipling oneself to be a disciple of Jesus means committing oneself to follow Jesus no matter where He leads. Since Jesus learned to endure hardness we must expect to experience and endure hardness as a good soldier also. Our experiences with Jesus Christ must affect our walk and commitment to Him, and these will have a profound affect upon our immediate families, neighborhoods and our nation.

I challenge you to re-examine your commitment to Jesus Christ and in prayer, ask the Holy Spirit to show you if you are a truly commited believer or a luke-warm "serving-when-it-is-convenient" believer. This book, *Radical Christian Living,* is a foundational and crystal clear teaching which is guaranteed to stir your heart to yearn for a successful fruit-bearing Christian life so that you can be an example wherever you go. The way of life of a true disciple of Jesus Christ is rough and tough at times, yet the sweet fellowship you will experience in His path is indescribable.

Dr. Paul Yonggi Cho, *Senior Pastor*
Yoido Full Gospel Church
Seoul, Korea

1

The Call to Discipleship

When we study the life and ministry of Jesus Christ, we quickly began to realize that He did not just seek converts. He did not just ask people to casually believe in Him. Nor did He call people to a religious organization or experience. He had something much more demanding in mind. Jesus called people to a way of life. He challenged men and women to forsake their own lives and follow Him. He called people to be His *disciples.* This is still His call today.

An Overlooked Ministry

Yet, in our Western brand of Christianity, we have somehow overlooked this aspect of the Christian life. *We have not seriously examined what it means to be a disciple of Jesus Christ.* Our presentation of the Gospel has, by and large, been so shallow that many who have responded to Christ have not truly realized the life-surrendering commitment to which He is calling them.

In addition, there has been only minimal follow-up with those who have responded to Christ. There has been even less true discipling of the believer. I'm afraid, that for the most part, baby Christians have been abandoned without the spiritual parenting that is absolutely necessary for them to grow to become mature disciples of Jesus Christ.

The result is that our churches in the West are filled with carnal minded people who are shallow in their knowledge of God, lukewarm in their commitment and have little or no impact on the world around them.

David Watson, in his excellent book, *Called and Committed,* wrote, "The vast majority of Western Christians— church members, pew-fillers, hymn-singers, sermon-tasters, Bible-readers, even born-again-believers or Spirit-filled-Charismatics, are not true disciples of Jesus. If we were willing to become disciples, the church in the West would be transformed, and the impact on society would be staggering" (Harold Shaw Publishers, 1982, page 2).

A recent Gallup poll reported that fifty million Americans claim to be Christians, and that this number is growing every year. This is a considerable part of the population of the United States. The *Christian influence of this many believers should have a profound impact on the moral standards of the nation.* But as we all sadly know, the level of morality in the United States has fallen so low that it is dangerously approaching the point of no return where God gives a people up to their own sins.

Cultural Christians

A further inquiry by the Gallup poll revealed that only *twelve per cent* of these fifty million Americans take their religious beliefs seriously enough that they have much affect on their lives. The poll confirmed what we all know but hate to admit, "The average American, including the Christian, is a biblical illiterate with a glaring lack of knowledge of even the basics of the Christian faith and with little spiritual discipline and consistency in his or her life" (Christian Life Magazine, May 1983). It's painfully obvious that most Americans are "cultural Christians" and not personal disciples of the Lord Jesus Christ.

Dr. Paul Yonggi Cho, who is pastor of the largest church in the world in Seoul, Korea was kind to write the foreword to this book. He has rightly observed that we Christians in the West spend too much time feasting and playing and not enough time fasting and praying.

Why I Wrote This Book

There is only one group of people who can save Western Civilization from further moral decay and the destruction of society that always accompanies it. That group is the church. *But first, there must be a great revival in the church.* This revival can only come as those who claim to be Christians seriously re-examine Christ's call to discipleship and then commit their life to Him accordingly.

I began to experience this revival and commitment to Christ in my own life in the early 1970's. I had made a "public profession" in Christ as a young boy while attending a church service. But acknowledging or accepting Jesus as your Savior is not necessarily the same as commiting your life to Him. Although I had "made a decision" for Jesus, I did not fully understand the signficance of His invitation to follow Him. It was many years later before I realized that Jesus called me and all who acknowledge Him as Lord to a way of life that was radically different from that of the world.

I wrote this book for the purpose of taking another look at the call Jesus gives to those who would bear His name. I write it in love out of a spirit that mourns over the condition of God's people. Yet, I also write it with faith and hope that God is going to send revival to the church and that we do have a glorious future.

A Look At What's Ahead

We're going to re-examine Christ's call to discipleship by answering five questions. Each question is answered in a separate chapter. The questions are:

1. *What is a disciple?*
2. *How do we become a disciple?*
3. *What is the cost of discipleship?*
4. *What are the marks of a disciple?*
5. *How do we make disciples?*

There is a review exercise at the end of the following chapters to help you highlight and reinforce what you have learned. The review exercises may be completed on an individual or group basis.

There are also some very helpful appendices at the back of the book. These give valuable practical information concerning Christian growth and training with a view of helping the believer become a mature disciple of Jesus Christ.

May God bless you now as you continue to read and help you to discover more clearly what it means to live as Christ's disciple. I pray that you'll not only apply the principles learned to your own life but will help others learn to live by them as well.

2

What Is A Disciple?

Before Jesus ascended to heaven, He gave a charge to His followers. We often speak of this charge as *"The Great Commission."* Jesus spoke these words, ". . . All authority has been given to Me in heaven and on earth. Go therefore and make disciples of all the nations, baptizing them in the name of the Father and of the Son and of the Holy Spirit, teaching them to observe all things whatever I have commanded you; and behold, I am with you always, even to the end of the age . . ." (Matthew 28:19-20 NKJ).

Please notice that Jesus said to make disciples (not converts). Of course, before we can make a disciple of someone else, we must first be a disciple ourself. So what is a disciple? A *disciple is a follower who learns from his teacher in order to imitate his teacher in word, thought and deed.* From this definition, we learn that a disciple is a follower, a learner and an imitator. He follows in order to learn—he learns in order to imitate.

Followers

Jesus called people to *follow Him*. It was at the Sea of Galilee where He initially put forth this challenge. Matthew records it for us. He said, " 'And Jesus, walking by the Sea of Galilee, saw two brothers, Simon called Peter, and Andrew his brother, casting a net into the sea; for they were fishermen. And He said to them, "Follow Me, and I will make you fishers of men." And they immediately left their nets and followed Him. And going on from there, He saw two other brothers, James the son of Zebedee, and John his brother, in the boat with Zebedee their father, mending their nets. And He called them, and immediately they left the boat and their father, and followed Him' " (Matthew 4:18-22 NKJ).

Luke adds that they forsook *all* and followed Him (Luke 5:11).

These men were fishermen. This is how they made their living. It was a family business. I'm sure their father spent many years of hard labor making the business prosperous. He taught his boys how to fish. He had great plans for them. No doubt, he was preparing them to take over the business when he retired.

But Jesus had a different plan for their lives. His plan was to make them fishers of men (Luke 5:10). He called them to leave the family business and abandon all their dreams, plans, aspirations and personal ambitions. Instead of following their own life plan; they were to follow Him. And I bet daddy wasn't too thrilled about their choice.

Likewise, God has a plan for your life. He makes His plan known to you when you follow Jesus Christ by appropriating Him as your Lord and walking in the Spirit. This is what Jesus meant when He said, ". . . I am the light of the world; he who follows me will not walk in darkness, but will have the light of life" (John 8:12 RSV).

God will give you light to see His divine plan for your life.

6

As He illuminates the pathway, you make whatever adjustments are necessary in your own life-plan to conform it to His. *Fulfilling God's plan for your life becomes your reason for living and gives meaning and purpose to all that you do.*

Adjusting Priorities

Now God has given all of us certain talents and abilities. And usually we have a job where we are able to use these God-given qualities. Normally, God wants you to remain on the job where He found you. But He wants to use you on that job to be a fisher of men and women. This usually requires that we make some adjustments in our priorities, attitudes and actions.

God probably won't ask you to literally leave your job as He did the first disciples. But He might. You must be willing to follow Him. *But I can assure you that whatever God asks you to do, He will first put the desire in your heart to do it.* God's plan will not be some grievous burden for you. Instead, as God puts the desire in your heart, whatever He asks you to do will be just what you want to do. You must be willing to be willing to follow Him. God will do the rest.

I can really identify with these first disciples. You see, when Jesus called me to follow Him, I was a businessman just as they were. I also had worked very hard and had built a successful professional career as a computer scientist and management consultant. Instead of casting nets, I trained managers how to use computers and computer personnel how to communicate with managers. But just as Jesus called Peter, Andrew, James and John to leave their nets, He also called me to leave my career for a full-time ministry of teaching the Bible and helping others learn to follow Him.

This change from computers to Christ took place over a period of several years. So it was no surprise to my wife, Peggy, when I came home one day and announced to her that I was leaving my good paying job with the oil company here in Houston. At that time, we had no bonds to cash, no stocks to sell, no savings to draw from, and now without the company benefits, there would be no insurance, hospital-ization or any other financial benefits we Americans are accustomed to having. And neither would there be a regular paycheck. As you can imagine, we had a lot of priorities to adjust. And even though a lot of well-meaning folks suggested that I was really making a foolish decision, I had to follow what I believed was the call of Jesus for my life.

Learners

Jesus calls us to follow Him because He leads us to God. As we listen to His words and observe His life, we learn the mind, heart and ways of God. God said through the prophet Isaiah, "Seek the Lord while he may be found, call upon him while he is near; let the wicked forsake his way, and the unrighteous man his thoughts; let him return to the Lord, that he may have mercy on him, and to our God, for he will abundantly pardon. For my thoughts are not your thoughts, neither are your ways my ways, says the Lord. For as the heavens are higher than the earth, so are my ways higher than your ways and my thoughts than your thoughts" (Isaiah 55:6-9 RSV).

God is not like His human creatures. His character is different from ours. His ways are different from our ways. His thoughts are not our thoughts. But He has supremely revealed Himself to us through Jesus Christ Who said, ". . . He who has seen Me has seen the Father . . ." (John 14:9 NKJ).

When God raised up Moses as a prophet, He told Moses that one would come in the future who would be the perfect prophet or spokesman for God. God said to Moses, "I will raise up for them a prophet like you from among their brethren; and I will put my words in his mouth, and he shall speak to them all that I command him. And whoever will not give heed to my words which he shall speak in my name, I myself will require it of him" (Deuteronomy 18:18-19 RSV).

Jesus claimed to be this prophet. He said, ". . . He who believes in Me, believes not in Me but in Him who sent Me. And he who sees Me sees Him who sent Me. I have come as

8

a light into the world, that whoever believes in Me should not abide in darkness. And if anyone hears My words, and does not believe, I do not judge him; for I did not come to judge the world but to save the world. He who rejects Me, and does not receive My words, has that which judges him—the word that I have spoken will judge him in the last day. For I have not spoken on My own authority; but the Father who sent Me gave Me a command, what I should say and what I should speak. And I know that His command is everlasting life. Therefore, whatever I speak, just as the Father said to Me, so I speak" (John 12:44-50 NKJ).

So we follow Jesus to learn the things of God. He not only gives us God's Word, but He Himself was the Word of God in the flesh. This means that God fully and completely revealed Himself to us through the life and ministry of Jesus Christ. (See John 5:36; 8:18; 14:8-11.)

Renewing Our Minds

As we follow Him, the Holy Spirit will enlighten our minds to help us know God and learn how to walk in His ways. Jesus said, "But the Helper, the Holy Spirit, whom the Father will send in My name, He will teach you all things, and bring to your remembrance all things that I said to you" (John 14:26 NKJ).

Jesus also said of the Holy Spirit, "However, when He, the Spirit of truth, has come, He will guide you into all truth; for He will not speak on His own authority, but whatever He hears He will speak; and He will tell you things to come. He will glorify Me, for He will take of what is Mine and declare it to you. All things that the Father has are Mine. Therefore I said He will take of Mine and declare it to you" (John 16:13-15 NKJ).

We learn the things of God by following Jesus Christ and walking in the Spirit. This is why Paul wrote, "I beseech you therefore, brethren, by the mercies of God, that you present your bodies a living sacrifice, holy, acceptable to God, which is your reasonable service. And do not be conformed to this world, but be transformed by the renewing of your

9

mind, that you may prove what is that good and acceptable and perfect will of God" (Romans 12:1-2 NKJ).

After leaving my career, I devoted eight to ten hours a day studying God's Word. The more I learned, the more I wanted to learn. And the more I wanted to learn, the deeper God took me in His Word. The desire to know God and learn to walk in His ways became my reason for living. My attitude became the same as the Apostle Paul who considered his past honors and accomplishments as dung compared to the priceless gain of knowing Christ.

Peggy was happy about this because she thought I would now give more attention to her and less to Monday night football which previously had been one of my favorite ways to pass the time. But she soon realized that Jesus had taken the place of Monday night football, so she began to read her Bible while I studied mine. We were both learning the things of God as the Holy Spirit began to renew our minds.

Imitators

We follow Jesus in order to learn from Jesus. We learn from Jesus in order to *imitate Him.* The word imitate means to act like in word, thought and deed.

Children always imitate their father. Sometimes this can be good, but sometimes it can be very embarrassing. As we have just learned, Jesus imitated His heavenly Father. Everything He thought, said and did was in the character of God. This is why God said of Jesus, ". . . This is My beloved Son, in whom I am well pleased" (Matthew 3:17 NKJ).

By Word and Example

Jesus taught His followers in two ways. *He taught by word and by example.* What He taught by His words, He lived out through His life. Jesus was a walking, living, breathing theological seminary. As the disciples heard Jesus teach, they also saw Him demonstrate His teachings through His life. (See Acts 1:1). He was the example and role model after which they were to pattern their own lives. They would be able to do this through the power of the Holy Spirit Who would live the life of Jesus through them. *They, in turn, would be examples for others to follow, learn from and imitate.*

Divine Copycats

Paul often reminded his followers about how he lived before them as an example for them to imitate. He wrote to the Christians at Corinth, "Be imitators of me, as I am of Christ" (1 Corinthians 11:1 RSV).

To the Philippian Christians, he said, "Brethren, join in imitating me, and mark those who so live as you have an example in us" (Philippians 3:17 RSV).

He reminded the Thessalonians with these words, "And you became imitators of us and of the Lord . . ." (1 Thessalonians 1:6 RSV). (See also 2 Thessalonians 3:9.)

Paul did not speak this way about himself in a self-righteous "holier-than-thou" attitude. But since he lived out what he taught, he was able in humility and good conscience, to point to himself as an example for the other Christians to observe.

Furthermore, he encouraged them to also be examples. He wrote to Timothy, "Let no one despise your youth, but be an example to the believers in word, in conduct, in love, in spirit, in faith, in purity" (1 Timothy 4:12 NKJ).

He encouraged the Ephesians Christians with these words, "Therefore be imitators of God, as beloved children" (Ephesians 5:1 RSV).

We too are to teach people about God by sharing with them His Word and living it out before them. We are God's living letters (2 Corinthians 3:1-3). As we walk with God, the Holy Spirit transforms us into the image of Jesus Christ (2 Corinthians 3:18). His life is reproduced in us.

Keeping Your Eyes on Jesus

People need to see examples of the Christian life being lived out before them. They would rather see a sermon than hear one. We instinctively recognize this and often piously tell people to "keep your eyes on Jesus."

But where is Jesus? He is physically in heaven. If people were to look up into the sky to see Him, they wouldn't be able to, unless God gave them some special vision of heaven. So how are they going to see Jesus? They are going to see Him as He lives out His life on planet Earth through His spiritual body—the Church. *They are going to see Him as His life is reproduced in you!*

If you are a Christian, how are your friends and acquaintances going to know about God's holiness unless they see it in you? How will they know about God's righteousness unless you live a righteous life before them? How will they know that God is love unless His love is flowing out of you? How will they know that God is good unless they see His goodness in you?

Salt and Light

We Christians are the God containers on planet Earth. Jesus lives His life through us. As the life of Christ is reproduced in us by the Holy Spirit, we have two effects on those around us. Jesus said we would be *salt and light.*

Here are His words in Matthew 5:13: "You are the salt of the earth; but if the salt loses its flavor, how shall it be seasoned? It is then good for nothing but to be thrown out and trampled under foot by men? (NKJ).

Our bodies require a certain amount of water in order to be healthy. As we eat salt, we become thirsty. This creates within us a desire to drink water. *Likewise, as the life of Jesus Christ is reproduced in us, it will create within others a thirst and desire to drink of the living waters of life that only Jesus can provide.* This will make them healthy spiritually, physically and emotionally.

Jesus went on to say, "You are the light of the world. A city that is set on a hill cannot be hidden. Nor do they light a lamp and put it under a basket, but on a lampstand, and it gives light to all who are in the house. Let your light so shine before men, that they may see your good works and glorify your Father who is in heaven" (Matthew 5:14-16 NKJ).

Light has two basic functions—life and sight. The Bible

says that without Christ, people are dead in their trespasses and sins and are blinded spiritually (Ephesians 2:1,5; 2 Corinthians 4:4). But when we walk as children of light, (Ephesians 5:8) they will see their need for Christ and receive His eternal life as they are born again (from above) by the Holy Spirit.

As we follow Jesus and humbly learn from Him, His life is reproduced in us. Those around us will see that life and want what we have. We then will be able to reproduce that same life in others. May all of us who are believers sincerely and humbly be able to say to our friends and acquaintances. *"Imitate me as I imitate Christ."*

Perhaps you consider yourself to be a disciple of Jesus Christ. I pray that you are and humbly ask you to examine yourself. Are you following Him? Are you learning His ways? Are you reproducing His life in others? Do others see Jesus in you? Are you living as salt and light? I know it is God's will for you to commit yourself to Him totally. I'm wanting more of that commitment in my own life. *Will you make that commitment too?*

Chapter 2—What is a Disciple?

Review Exercise

1. Write out a definition of the word "disciple".

2. List and briefly describe in your own words the three aspects of discipleship.

    a.

    b.

    c.

3. How can you apply this knowledge to your own life?

3

How Do We Become A Disciple?

The second question we want to answer in this book is how do we become a disciple? There is really one requirement. But it is a requirement to which few are willing to commit. The requirement is *self-death*. We must die to our self-life.

The word *self-life* refers to our own personal soulish life-plan. Before we become Jesus' disciple, this life-plan is naturally centered around us rather than Him. It is based on our dreams, our plans, our aspirations and our ambitions. But once we become Jesus' disciple, we're going to follow His plan for our life. And His plan for our life is not going to be the same as our plan. *So to die to ourselves, simply means we willingly lay aside our life-plan for His.*

Jesus, of course, set this example for us. He said, "For I came down from heaven, not to do My own will, but the will of Him who sent Me" (John 6:38 NKJ).

He calls His disciples to do the same. Jesus said to all who would follow Him, ". . . If anyone desires to come after Me, let him deny himself, take up his cross daily, and follow Me. For whoever desires to save his life will lose it, but whoever loses his life for My sake will save it" (Luke 9:23-24 NKJ).

Jesus spoke about taking up our cross daily. Many people misunderstand what Jesus meant by this. They think He was talking about them having to bear some heavy burden to the point of suffering for Jesus' sake. But this is not at all what He meant.

To understand the meaning of Jesus' words, we must place ourselves in His time period and understand Him as His listeners would have understood Him. If you lived in Jesus' time and saw someone carrying his own cross, you knew that person was going to die. Likewise, to *"take up your cross daily" means to die to yourself.*

Dying to Live

Paul wrote to the Galatian Christians that he was dead to the world and the world was dead to him (Galatians 6:14). By that, he meant that he no longer cared for his own personal worldly ambitions. He no longer coveted the world's applause, praise, awards, honors and glory. *He only coveted the things of God.* He only desired to follow Jesus and walk in His divine life-plan. At the same time, the world system no longer cared to honor Paul. As far as it was concerned, Paul was dead.

Paul summarized this self-death requirement with these words, "I have been crucified with Christ; it is no longer I who live, but Christ who lives in me; and the life I now live in the flesh I live by faith in the Son of God, who loved me and gave himself for me" (Galatians 2:20 RSV).

A Modern Example

We in the western world are both amazed and alarmed at the rapid growth and threat of modern communism. The reason why communism has spread throughout the world in such a short period of time is because those who believe and preach its message have practiced the biblical principle of dying to self.

Keith Green Ministries published a gospel tract called *Communism Verses Christianity*. In the tract, they share the following true story.

A young American college student was engaged to be married. He and his fiancé had made great plans and eagerly looked ahead to their future together. During the time of this engagement, the young man was converted to communism. He became so devoted to the communist cause that he wrote a letter to his fiancé in which he broke off their engagement.

His letter reads as follows:

"We Communists have a high casualty rate. We're the ones who get slandered and ridiculed and fired from our jobs and in every other way made as uncomfortable as possible. A certain percentage of us get killed or imprisoned. We live in virtual poverty. We turn back to the Party every penny we make above what is absolutely necessary to keep us alive. We Communists don't have time or the money for many movies or concerts or T-bone steaks or decent homes and new cars. We've been described as fanatics. We are fanatics! Our lives are dominated by one great overshadowing factor, the struggle for World Communism.

"We Communists have a philosophy of life which no amount of money could buy. We have a cause to fight for, a definite purpose in life. We subordinate our petty, personal selves into a great movement of humanity. And if our personal lives seem hard or our egos appear to suffer through subordination to the Party, then we are adequately compensated by the fact that each of us in his small way is contributing to something new and true and better for mankind.

"The Communist cause is my life, my business, my religion, my hobby, my sweetheart, my wife and mistress, my bread and meat. I work at it in the daytime and dream of it at night. Its hold on me grows, not lessens, as time goes on. Therefore, I cannot carry on a friendship, a love affair, or even a conversation without relating it to this force which both guides and drives my life. I evaluate people, books, ideas and actions according to how they affect the Communist cause and by their attitude toward it. I've already been in jail because of my ideas, and if necessary, I'm ready to go before a firing squad."

The letter exemplifies the meaning of dying to self. The young man laid aside his personal life and gave himself completely to the counterfeit gospel of communism. Surely we Christians should do the same for the true liberating gospel of Jesus Christ.

In his book, *The Cross and Sanctification,* T. A. Hegre included the following Communist indictment of uncommitted Christians. Read it and weep!

"The Gospel is a much more powerful weapon for the renewal of society than is our Marxist philosophy; but all the same, it is we who will finally beat you. We are only a handful, and you Christians are numbered by the million; but if you remember the story of Gideon and his three hundred companions, you will understand that I am right.

We Communists do not play with words. We are realists and seeing that we are determined to achieve our object, we know how to obtain the means. Of our salaries and wages, we keep only that which is strictly necessary, and we give up the rest for propaganda purposes. To this propaganda we also "consecrate" all our free time, and a part of our holidays. You, however, give only a little time and hardly any money for the spreading of the gospel of Christ.

How can you believe in the supreme value of this gospel if you do not practice it, if you do not spread it, and if you sacrifice neither time nor money for it?

Believe me, it is we who will win, for we believe in our Communist message, and we are ready to sacrifice everything, even our life, in order that social justice shall triumph; but you people are afraid to soil your hands."

Letting Go of Self

I once heard a humorous story that well illustrates the problem we all have of self-death. It goes like this. A man slipped off the edge of a steep cliff and was falling to his death. He somehow managed to grab hold of a tree branch to which he clung with all of his might. Desperately, he cried out to God, "God! If you are really up there, please help me." A voice came back from heaven and said to the man, *"Let go of the branch."* The man, knowing that he would surely fall to his death if he let go of the branch replied, "Is there anybody else up there?"

I'm sure you see the point of this little story. The branch represents our old self-life. We cling to it with all our might. We're afraid to let go. We're afraid to trust God. Because we don't really know Him as we should, we're afraid He might let us fall. While all along God is saying, *"Let go of the old self-life.* Trust Me to have your best interest at heart."

Jesus said it this way, "Most assuredly, I say to you, unless a grain of wheat falls into the ground and dies, it remains alone; but if it dies, it produces much grain. He who loves his life will lose it, and he who hates his life in this world will keep it for life eternal" (John 12:24-25 NKJ).

Contribution or Commitment?

This self-death requirement demands that we commit ourselves completely to the Lordship of Jesus Christ in every area of our life. It seems that many professing Christians only desire to make a contribution to the kingdom of God, but they are not willing to really commit their lives to it. Let me tell you a little story to explain the difference between a contribution and a commitment.

There was a chicken and pig who were good friends. One

19

day as they were walking together, the chicken noticed an advertisement in the window of a restaurant. The advertisement read, "Bacon and eggs—all you can eat for $1.00." Feeling somewhat generous, the chicken turned to the pig and said, "Let's go in and make a contribution." To that, the pig replied, "You are only going to make a contribution, but I'll have to make a commitment."

Well, the chicken had in mind laying a few eggs and then going on his own way. But the pig was going to have to give his life. Do you see the difference? Many professing Christians are like the chicken. They only want to make a contribution to the kingdom of God. They lay a few eggs (religious activities) and think they have done their duty and pleased God. But God isn't pleased. He is not interested in our contribution to His kingdom. He wants us to commit our lives to it. *God doesn't want anything you have—He wants you!*

One time a close friend came to me for counseling. He and his pastor, who was also a close friend of mine, were having some problems communicating with each other and agreeing on priorities. I related the chicken and pig story to my friend and encouraged him to examine his own heart concerning the problem at hand. He thought about it to himself for a few minutes and then with a facetious grin declared that he was part chicken and part pig. Of course he realized this was impossible. He was either one or the other.

What about you, dear reader. *Are you making a contribution or a commitment?* Perhaps you have been one who has been content just making contributions to the kingdom of God. But you have never really committed your life to it. It is my prayer that you will make that commitment and give yourself completely to become Jesus' disciple. But as much as I hope you will make that decision, I *must first warn you to count the cost that it involves.*

Chapter 3—How do We Become a Disciple?

Review Exercise

1. What is the one requirement to be a disciple of Jesus Christ? Explain!

2. What does it mean to "take up your cross daily?" Explain!

3. How can you apply this knowledge to your own life?

4

What Is The Cost of Discipleship?

It was Jesus Himself who told us to count the cost before becoming His disciple. Luke records the following account, "And there went great multitudes with Him (Jesus). And He turned and said to them, 'If anyone comes to Me and does not hate his father and mother, wife and children, brothers and sisters, yes and his own life also, he cannot be My disciple. And whoever does not bear his cross and come after Me cannot be My disciple' " (Luke 14:25-27 NKJ).

A big crowd was following Jesus. They had seen Him perform many miracles. Many of the people were nothing more than curiosity seekers. Others were following Him for selfish reasons. They just wanted Him to meet their own personal needs. They weren't really committed to Him.

A Challenge to the Crowd

So Jesus spoke to them about the need for commitment. He looked at that big crowd and knew that the vast majority of the people did not understand the commitment to which He was calling them. Furthermore, He also knew that once they did understand, they would no longer follow Him.

Jesus didn't want them to be mislead. *So He told them that whoever followed Him must love Him more than anyone else.* This would include the person's most cherished relationship such as his own family members and even the person's own life, as well. *Their relationship to Him would be more important than any earthly relationship.* This is the meaning of the Greek word which is translated into English as "hate." (See also Matthew 10:34–39.) It was like Jesus was saying to the crowds, "Before you hitch your wagon to me, let's make something very clear . . . First, count the cost."

Jesus then gives two examples about counting the cost. The first is about a builder. The second a king. He says, "For which of you, intending to build a tower, does not sit down first and count the cost, whether he has enough to finish it—lest, after he has laid the foundation, and is not able to finish, all who see it begin to mock him, saying, 'This man began to build and was not able to finish.' Or what king, going to war against another king, does not sit down first and consider whether he is able to meet him who comes against him with twenty thousand? Or else, while the other is still a great way off, he sends a delegation and asks conditions of peace" (Luke 14:28-32 NKJ).

In both of these examples, Jesus was teaching the necessity of counting the cost before making a decision. He knew the crowd of would-be followers had not done this concerning their relationship to Him. Now that He has them thinking about it, He quickly makes His point, "So likewise, whoever of you does not forsake all that he has, he cannot be My disciple" (Luke 14:33 NKJ).

The Prosperity Christian

Luke also tells us about three who came to Jesus wanting to be His disciples. But they had not counted the cost. Luke writes about the first man, "And it came to pass, as they went on the road, a certain man said to Him, 'Lord, I will follow You wherever You go.' And Jesus said to him, 'Foxes have holes and birds of the air have nests, but the Son of Man has nowhere to lay His head' " (Luke 9:57-58 NKJ).

This man thought he wanted to follow Jesus. He had heard, no doubt, that Jesus was going to establish a kingdom. He thought this was going to be a physical kingdom. He wanted to be part of this physical kingdom because it would mean material prosperity for him. Jesus pointed out that He had no material prosperity to offer the person. In fact, He didn't even have a house to call His own. He stayed in other people's houses or slept in the open. This man wanted to follow Jesus for what he could get from Him. He had not counted the cost of material comforts.

It seems that a lot of people today are like this man. They follow Jesus for what they think He can do for them. They are only interested in themselves. *Their's is a "gimme-gimme" relationship to Jesus. If God doesn't instantly meet their every self-centered demand, their hearts grow cold.* They are not prepared for hardships. They are not willing to make sacrifices. They haven't counted the cost of material comforts.

When I think about counting the cost of material comforts, I'm reminded of the incredible faithfulness of God in meeting my needs. Peggy and I have not had a known income in years. Yet, God has always been faithful to provide us with the finances we have needed when we needed them. We still live in the same house, we haven't missed a meal, all our bills are paid, and we don't owe a penny to anyone. Isn't God good!

The Self-Sufficient Christian

Now let's consider the second man who came to Jesus. Luke writes, "And He said to another, 'Follow Me.' But he said, 'Lord, let me first go and bury my father.' Jesus said to him, 'Let the dead bury their own dead, but you go and preach the kingdom of God' " (Luke 9:59-60 NKJ).

This is an interesting situation. To properly understand this man's concern, we must relate it to Jewish customs and practices that were common during the time of Jesus. One such custom was that the first-born stayed home until his father died. He would then bury his father and receive his inheritance. *Then he would be self-sufficient and not have to depend on anyone.*

This could very well be the situation with this man. If so, he was telling Jesus that he wanted to wait until he was self-sufficient before he followed him. In this way, he would have enough money to take care of himself and not have to depend on anyone—including Jesus.

And you know, there are many Christians like that today. They'll follow Jesus up to a point. But they will never put themselves in a position where they actually have to depend on Him and trust Him. They are self-sufficient. They've got their financial security blankets to cover them in times of crisis. *They have "in God we trust" written on their money, but it's really their money they have put their trust in.* They don't need anyone—including Jesus. They haven't counted the cost of total dependence on God.

A Christian brother called me on the phone one day to discuss the possibility of publishing one of my books. I explained to him how God had earlier called me to leave my successful career to serve Him full-time as a teacher and writer. I went into great detail explaining to him how I live by faith on a day-to-day basis totally depending on God to meet my needs. Yet, even after explaining this, his immediate reply was that I must be living on a retirement income that I had stored away somewhere. He thought I had to be self-sufficient. After I explained again so that he clearly understood, he got on a plane and came to visit me to see for himself. We can depend totally on God and trust Him as our source.

The Family Christian

Then there's the third man who came to Jesus. Luke writes, "And another also said, 'Lord, I will follow You, but let me first go bid them farewell who are at my house.' And Jesus said to him, 'No one, having put his hand to the plow, and looking back, is fit for the kingdom of God' " (Luke 9:61-62 NKJ).

Now what was this man's problem? His problem was that he was more concerned with what his daddy thought than he was with Jesus' call to follow Him. He wanted to ask his father's permission to follow Jesus. He put his father's authority over Jesus' authority. *He did not count the cost of family rejection.* Therefore, Jesus rejected him.

Many Christians in our modern world have the same problem. They would like to follow Jesus, but not if it's going to cause problems within the family. *They are more concerned with their family relationships than they are their relationship with God.* This becomes a barrier keeping them from being Jesus' disciple.

I remember how hard it was to explain to my relatives why I was leaving my career and what I believed God wanted me to do. Some must have thought I was "throwing away" my past education and accomplishments and were disappointed that I wasn't going to be what they thought I should be or wanted me to be. Others just couldn't understand what I was going to do and were genuinely concerned for our future. So was I! But I knew that following God's will for my life, even though I didn't know where it would lead me, was the most important thing in my life.

These are just three representative cases of people who wanted to be Jesus' disciples but had not counted the cost. One was not willing to sacrifice financially. Another wanted to be self-sufficient. The third put his family first. Beloved reader, is there anything that is keeping you from being Jesus' disciple? If there is, *I pray that you will count the cost and accept His call to discipleship to be the most important consideration in your life. Will you make that decision now?*

Chapter 4—What is the Cost of Discipleship?

Review Exercise

1. What is the cost of discipleship?

2. How did Jesus challenge the crowd of would-be followers?

3. How can you apply this knowledge to your own life?

5

What Are The Marks Of A Disciple?

Many people claim to be disciples of Jesus Christ. But just saying it doesn't make it a fact. The person must demonstrate it in his or her life. *I believe the Bible teaches six qualities in a person's life that mark that person as a true disciple of Jesus Christ.* Jesus, as our example, demonstrated these in His own life. And He requires each of His disciples to follow His example. These six qualities are as follows.

Love

The first mark of one who is a disciple of Jesus Christ is *love.* Jesus loved. Paul wrote, "Therefore be imitators of God, as beloved children. And walk in love, as Christ loved us and gave himself up for us, a fragrant offering and sacrifice to God" (Ephesians 5:1-2 RSV).

Jesus said, "A new commandment I give to you, that you love one another; as I have loved you, that you also love one another. By this all will know that you are My disciples, if you have love for one another" (John 13:34-35 NJK).

The Greek word for love in this verse is *agape*. It is a God given love that we do not naturally have. God's kind of love is an uncaused love that has been poured into our hearts by the Holy Spirit. It enables us to love others unconditionally and includes our enemies as well as our friends.

Jesus said this directive to love was a new commandment. The commandment itself wasn't new because God gave it to the Hebrews 1500 years earlier. (See Leviticus 19:18,34.) But what made this commandment new was the quality or type of love with which we would be loving. *We would be loving others as Christ loved us with an unconditional, uncaused sacrificial love.*

Jesus says that His agape love is the true mark of His disciples. The apostle John put it this way, "Beloved, let us love one another, for love is of God; and everyone who loves is born of God and knows God. He who does not love does not know God, for God is love . . . And we have known and believed the love that God has for us. God is love, and he who dwells in love dwells in God, and God in Him" (1 John 4:7-8,16 NKJ).

John then adds, "If someone says, 'I love God,' and hates his brother, he is a liar; for he who does not love his brother whom he has seen, how can he love God whom he has not seen? And this commandment we have from Him: that he who loves God loves his brother also' " (1 John 4:20-21 NKJ).

Many people may say that they love Jesus. Many people may say they love you. *But the proof is in their attitude and actions.* John put it so well. He said, "My little children, let us not love in word or in tongue, but in deed and in truth" (1 John 3:18 NKJ).

Fruit Bearing

The second mark of a true disciple of Jesus Christ is he *bears fruit.* This is the fruit of the Spirit. Jesus bore fruit. In fact, the fruit of the Spirit is simply the very character and life of Jesus being lived out of us by the Holy Spirit. Thus, fruit bearing is a true test of a person's relationship with Jesus Christ.

Jesus said it in these words, "I am the true vine, and My Father is the vinedresser. Every branch in Me that does not bear fruit He takes away; and every branch that bears fruit He prunes, that it may bear more fruit. You are already clean because of the word which I have spoken to you. Abide in Me, and I in you. As the branch cannot bear fruit of itself, unless it abides in the vine, neither can you, unless you abide in Me. I am the vine, you are the branches. He who abides in Me and I in Him, bears much fruit; for without Me you can do nothing. If anyone does not abide in Me, he is cast out as a branch and is withered; and they gather them and throw them into the fire, and they are burned. If you abide in Me, and My words in you, you shall ask what you desire, and it shall be done for you. By this My Father is glorified, that you bear much fruit; so you will be My disciples" (John 15:1-8 NKJ).

Jesus then adds, "You have not chosen me, but I have chosen you and appointed you that you should go and bear fruit, and that your fruit should remain . . ." (John 15:16 NKJ).

Jesus warned us against people who profess to be Christians but bear no fruit. His words were, "Beware of false prophets, who come to you in sheep's clothing, but inwardly they are ravenous wolves. You will know them by their fruits. Do men gather grapes from thornbushes or figs from thistles? Even so, every good tree bears good fruit, but a bad tree bears bad fruit. A good tree cannot bear bad fruit, nor can a bad tree bear good fruit. Every tree that does not bear good fruit is cut down and thrown into the fire. Therefore, by their fruits you will know them" (Matthew 7:15-20 NKJ).

The test of a disciple of Jesus is not that the person understands everything about the Bible, can debate doctrines of the faith, perform miracles, sing in the choir, or teach a Sunday school class. *The test is fruit bearing.*

Obedience

The third mark or quality of a disciple of Jesus Christ is *obedience.* Jesus obeyed the Father. He said, ". . . I always do those things that please Him" (John 8:29 NKJ). On another occasion, Jesus said, "My food (nourishment) is to do the will of Him who sent Me, and to finish His work" (John 4:34 NKJ).

Jesus expects no less of His disciples. He had been preaching and many believed in Him. But He wanted them to know that believing must be evidenced by obedience. So He stopped in the middle of His sermon and said, ". . . If you continue in My word, then you are My disciples indeed" (John 8:31 NKJ).

Jesus coupled obedience with love. He told His disciples, "If you love Me, keep My commandments . . . He who has My commandments and keeps them, it is he who loves Me" (John 14:15,21 NKJ).

On one occasion, Jesus gave a rebuke. He said, "And why do you call Me 'Lord, Lord,' and do not do the things which I say" (Luke 6:46 NKJ).

He went on to say, "Not everyone who says to Me, 'Lord, Lord,' will enter the kingdom of heaven, but he who does the will of My Father who is in heaven. Many will say to Me in that day, 'Lord, Lord, have we not prophesied in Your name, cast out demons in Your name and done many wonderful works in Your name?' And then I will declare to them, 'I never knew you; depart from Me, you who practice lawlessness" (Matthew 7:21-23 NKJ).

Jesus then gave them an example to illustrate His point. He said, "Therefore whoever hears these saying of Mine, and does them, I will liken him to a wise man who built his house on the rock: and the rain descended, the floods came, and the winds blew and beat on that house; and it did not fall, for it was founded on the rock. And everyone who hears these sayings of Mine, and does not do them, will be like a foolish man who built his house on the sand: and the rain descended, the floods came, and the winds blew and beat on that house; and it fell. And great was its fall!" (Matthew 7:24-27).

The Word of God is not just to be learned; it is to be obeyed. If we really love God and want to follow Jesus, we will learn what He wants us to do and then we will do it. Not everyone who sings "He is Lord" is a disciple of Jesus. *Not everyone who attends church meetings or goes to a Bible study is a disciple of Jesus. A disciple of Jesus Christ obeys Jesus Christ.* As the apostle James wrote, "Be ye doers of the word, and not hearers only . . ." (James 1:22 KJV).

Submission

A disciple of Jesus Christ also *submits* to Jesus Christ. Submission is different from obedience. *Obedience refers to outward acts. Submission relates to heart attitudes.* A person can be obedient and not submissive. He can perform an outward act but be doing it with a hard heart. On the other hand, he can be submissive and not obedient. This would be a situation in which a person must refuse to obey an ungodly instruction but would do so with a humble spirit. *A disciple is both obedient and submissive to the Lordship of Jesus Christ.* He not only obeys, but he does so joyfully from his heart.

Jesus submitted to His heavenly Father. The night Jesus was taken captive, He was agonizing over the events He was soon to face. Not only was He going to be beaten unmercifully, profoundly humiliated and crucified, but even worse, for the first time in all eternity, He was going to be separated from His heavenly Father. Yet He prayed, "O My Father, if it is possible, let this cup pass from Me; nevertheless, not as I will, but as You will" (Matthew 26:39 NKJ).

Jesus not only obeyed, but He joyfully submitted to the will of His heavenly Father. As our example, the writer of Hebrews says we should be "looking to Jesus, the author and finisher of our faith, who for the joy that was set before Him endured the cross, despising the shame, and has sat down at the right hand of the throne of God" (Hebrews 12:2 NKJ).

Regarding submission, Jesus said, "Come to Me, all you who labor and are heavy laden, and I will give you rest. Take My yoke upon you and learn from Me, for I am gentle and lowly in heart, and you will find rest for your souls. For My yoke is easy and My burden is light" (Matthew 11:28-30 NKJ).

The yoke was used to couple two things together. In ancient times it was placed on the necks of the conquered showing their servitude to their new masters (Jeremiah 27:2; 28:13). It was a sign of submission to authority.

We who have been coupled to Jesus Christ by the Holy Spirit are to submit to His authority over our lives. It takes many Christians a life time and some never realize, that Jesus is more than just our friend who desires to bless us and help us out when we get in trouble. *Jesus came to take over our lives.* Our relationship to Him is one of Lord and servant. He is the master, ruler, and controller of our life. Therefore, we submit to His authority, joyfully doing those things that please Him.

We not only submit to Christ directly, but also indirectly through our attitudes towards others. This means we are to have a humble and meek spirit towards Christ, all our Christian family and even to those who do not profess to know Christ.

The writer of Hebrews says, "Obey those who have the rule over you, and submit yourselves, for they watch out for your souls, as those who must give account. Let them do it with joy and not with grief, for that would be unprofitable for you" (Hebrews 13:17 NKJ).

Paul wrote in Ephesians, "Honor Christ by submitting to each other" (Ephesians 5:21 TLB).

Peter said, "Therefore submit yourselves to every ordinance of man for the Lord's sake . . ." (1 Peter 2:13 NKJ). (See also 1 Peter 2:18;3:1-5;5:5).

Many Christians want to be in positions of authority. But they are not willing to submit to authority nor Godly counsel from others. They think they are "free spirits" who can do their own thing and need no one but Jesus to guide them. This sounds so spiritual—but it's not. Jesus guides us directly but also through those around us.

This does not mean blind obedience. All relationships are "as unto the Lord." God never expects us to obey an instruction that is contrary to Scripture. (See Acts 5:29). But He does expect us to have a humble spirit, even if we're not able to obey an instruction that we know is not from God. Remember—God is interested in our heart attitudes, as well as our outward acts.

We must learn to receive authority before we can excercise it. *We must learn to take orders before we can give them.* We do this by demonstrating a humble attitude and teachable spirit in our relationships with one another. If at all possible, every disciple of Jesus Christ should be attached to a local expression of the body of Christ and in submission to all the members of that fellowship of believers. This is one way we submit to Christ's authority in our lives.

Servanthood

Another mark of a disciple of Jesus Christ is *servanthood.* Jesus served. At the last supper Jesus had with His disciples, they had been arguing over who was going to be the greatest in His kingdom. Jesus needed some dramatic way to demonstrate that the road to greatness was through servanthood. So He rose from His place at the head of the table. Then He took off His master's robe, put on a towel which was the dress of a servant and washed their feet. That ended the argument as they were all stunned and silenced by Jesus' act.

After Jesus washed their feet, He said, "You call me Teacher and Lord, and you say well, for so I am. If I then, your Lord and Teacher, have washed your feet, you also ought to wash one another's feet. For I have given you an example, that you should do as I have done to you. Most assuredly, I say to you, a servant is not greater than his Master; nor is he who is sent greater than he who sent him. If you know these things, happy are you if you do them" (John 13:13-17 NKJ).

One day James and John's mother came to Jesus and asked Him to let her sons have special places of rule and authority in His kingdom. Well, the other disciples heard her and got mad. How could she ask such a thing, they thought? Jesus heard them arguing and used the situation to teach them how one comes to rule in the kingdom of God.

Matthew writes, "But Jesus called them to Himself and said, 'You know that the rulers of the Gentiles lord it over them, and those who are great exercise authority over them. Yet it shall not be so among you; but whoever desires to become great among you, let him be your servant. And whoever desires to be first among you, let him be your slave—just as the Son of Man did not come to be served, but to serve, and to give His life a ransom for many' " (Matthew 20:25-28 NKJ).

On another occasion, Jesus told the religious leaders, "But he who is greatest among you shall be your servant. And whoever exalts himself will be abased, and he who humbles himself will be exalted" (Matthew 23:11-12 NKJ).

The way to greatness in the kingdom of God is through servanthood. In fact, a disciple of Jesus Christ exercises his spiritual authority through serving. We Christians often speak about the freedom and liberty we have through Christ. I sometimes hear Christian friends quoting Galatians 5:1 where Paul writes, "Stand fast therefore in the liberty with which Christ has made us free, and do not be entangled again with a yoke of bondage" (NKJ).

Christ has set us free and this is fantastic. It's wonderful to be free in Jesus. *But why has He set us free?* Paul answers this question for us in the same chapter to the Galatian Christians. He says, "For you, brethren, have been called to liberty; only do not use liberty as an opportunity for the flesh, but by love serve one another" (Galatians 5:13 NKJ).

Paul reminds us of the purpose for which Christ has set us free. *He has freed us from ourselves that we, through love, might serve others.* As we serve others in Christ's body, we are actually serving Him. This is another reason why it is important to be physically attached to a local expression of His body. *We exercise our authority in the local church by serving the members of that local church. In this way, we serve Christ.*

This is a privilege God has given us. Jesus set the example. He expects us to follow that example and spiritually wash the feet of our Christian brothers and sisters by serving them in love. This is not only our privilege—it's our duty. It is the true mark of a disciple.

Jesus said it this way, "Will any one of you, who has a servant plowing or keeping sheep, say to him when he has come in from the field, 'Come at once and sit down at the table'? Will he not rather say to him, 'Prepare supper for me, and gird yourself and serve me, till I eat and drink; and afterward you shall eat and drink'? Does he thank the servant because he did what was commanded? So you also, when you have done all that is commanded you, say, 'We are unworthy servants; we have only done what was our duty' " (Luke 17:7-10 RSV).

Reproduction

The last mark or quality of a disciple of Jesus Christ is *reproduction.* Jesus reproduced His life in others. Jesus' followers were anxiously waiting for Him to establish His kingdom. As the time drew near, Jesus said, ". . . The hour has come that the Son of Man should be glorified. Most assuredly, I say to you, unless a grain of wheat falls into the ground and dies, it remains alone; but if it dies, it produces much grain. He who loves his life will lose it, and he who hates his life in this world will keep it to eternal life" (John 12:23-25 NKJ).

Jesus' followers expected Him to overthrow the Roman

Empire by force and establish a political kingdom on planet Earth. He is going to establish a political kingdom at His second coming. But the purpose of His first coming was to overthrow the kingdom of self that is within each of us and establish His rule in our hearts. His objective was to bring us forgiveness for our sins and reproduce His life in us. But He had to die in order to do it.

Since Jesus lived a perfect life and never knew sin, it was not necessary for Him to die. He could have bypassed the cross and ascended back to heaven. But He would have gone alone. He would have showed up empty handed. He would not have accomplished His objective.

So as He spoke about entering into His glory, He also talked about dying. He was the "grain of wheat" that would fall to the ground and die. But because He never knew sin, death could not hold Him in the grave. Therefore, He came forth victorious over death, walked planet Earth for forty days and appeared to many of His followers. Then He ascended back to heaven from where He sent the Holy Spirit to give us eternal life and reproduce His own life in us.

Jesus then says we are to follow His example of self-death in order to reproduce His life in others. He says those who love their life will lose it. The Greek word that is translated into this English word life is *psuche.* It refers to our soulish *self-life* which is self centered and seeks to do its own thing. As long as we try to hold on to this life, the life of Christ will not be produced in us nor reproduced in others. Furthermore, we'll lose this life in the end as God brings down all that is opposed to Him.

But to those who prefer not their psuche life, Jesus promises that they will have eternal life. The Greek word which is translated into this English word life is *Zoe.* This refers to the life of Jesus Christ coming to live in us through the Holy Spirit. *It is this God-kind of life that we want to reproduce in others.*

As we die to ourselves, the Holy Spirit lives the life of Jesus Christ in us. This life flows out of us towards others who will also want to receive Christ in them. In this way, we reproduce His life in those around us. They then become the disciple of Jesus in us. *We don't just bring them to Christ and leave them. But we give ourselves to them as Jesus gave Himself to us. We commit our life to them as He committed His life to us.* (See 1 Thessalonians 2:8). We teach them by word and example, and by so doing we say to them, "Follow, learn and imitate Christ in me."

This is what it means to live as Christ's disciple. We follow Him, learn from Him and imitate Him. His love flows out of us. We bear the fruit of His Spirit. We obey Him and submit to His authority. We serve Him. We die to ourselves so that His life might be reproduced through us in others. *We don't do this in isolation but through relationships that God has established between us and others in a local Christian community. As we live unto them; we are living unto Him.*

Do the six qualities discussed in this chapter describe your life? I certainly hope they do. I'm desiring that more of them will be seen in my own life. You can experience them personally by becoming a true disciple of Jesus Christ. As you draw near to God, He will draw near to you, and these qualities will develop in you as the Holy Spirit lives the very life of Jesus through you.

I've discovered in my own life that this is not an easy task. It certainly doesn't come naturally. When I first began to follow Jesus, I had a great zeal and a certain measure of spiritual authority and charisma. But I tried to beat people over the head with the Bible rather than leading them to Jesus through His uncaused love. As you can imagine, there wasn't a whole lot of fruit.

I did my best to obey God's Word, but I can't say I was always submissive, particularly to others who also has a certain measure of spiritual authority. My mind was not yet renewed, and like the first disciples, my concern was how to be the greatest in the kingdom rather than how to be the servant of all.

That was certainly not the attitude and life I wanted to reproduce in others. Hopefully my life now is a greater reflection of the character of Christ with His own God-kind of life more and more evident. My heart cries out with John the Baptist that Jesus in me would increase and self would decrease (see John 3:30).

Chapter 5—What are the Marks of a Disciple?

Review Exercise

1. List the six qualities of a disciple of Jesus Christ.

    a.
    b.
    c.
    d.
    e.
    f.

2. How can you apply this knowledge to your life?

6

How Do We Make Disciples?

As we've emphasized throughout this writing, Jesus calls us to be His disciples. We've learned what a disciple is, how to become a disciple, the cost of discipleship and the marks of a true disciple. It is my fervent prayer that you have or will enter into this relationship with Jesus Christ.

But even this is not all God desires for us. *For you see, Jesus not only calls us to be His disciples, He also commands us to make disciples of others.* This is the heart of the "Great Commission." Remember, He said, "Go and make disciples." If you have made a commitment to be Christ's disciple and are truly living out that commitment in your life, you now want to teach others how to do so, as well. In light of this, we're now going to learn how you can help others become disciples of Jesus Christ.

The Biblical Pattern

Jesus Himself is the model disciple maker. Therefore, the best way to learn how to make disciples is to see how Jesus did it. We can then pattern our approach after His. To help us understand the approach Jesus took, I have boiled it down to five steps. These are:

1. *Select*
2. *Commit*
3. *Teach*
4. *Assign*
5. *Send*

We're now going to study each of these steps and learn how we can apply them to our own ministry responsibility of disciple making.

1. Select

The first step Jesus took was that of *selection*. He had to select or choose from the great multitudes, a few who were to be His close companions and become His disciples. Jesus was a very realistic and practical person. He knew that the masses of people were easily swayed and needed close attention. Yet as just one individual, He could not personally give all of them the supervision they required. He also understood that "the crowd" would never change the world as He so desired. Knowing these things, *Jesus' strategy was to gather a few committed people around Him, teach them, pour His life into them, and then send them out to do the same in the lives of others as He had done in their life.* In this way, they would carry on the ministry after Jesus had to physically leave them. We learn from this that *Jesus' method of changing the world was not through bigger and better programs but through committed people.*

In view of this approach, the selection of those who were to be His disciples was the most critical step in the entire process. *The success of Jesus' very ministry depended on*

His choosing the right people to disciple. If He did not make a wise choice, there would be no lasting fruit and His ministry would be a failure.

Because this was so important, *Jesus spent much time in prayer seeking divine insight concerning His choice.* We read in Luke, "Now it came to pass in those days that He went out to the mountain to pray, and continued all night in prayer to God. And when it was day, He called His disciples to Him; and from them He chose twelve . . ." (Luke 6:12-13 NKJ).

Jesus chose the twelve only after much prayer. These were men He was divinely led to select. Although they were just ordinary people and would fail Him many times, Jesus had spiritual insight that they were the ones He was to choose. Jesus selected them because He believed they would respond to His teachings. Later on, Judas, who was one of the twelve, betrayed Jesus in fulfillment of Scripture which said the Messiah would be betrayed by a close friend (Psalm 41:9)

We notice that the number of men Jesus chose was small. There are different theories as to why He chose twelve. The theological significance of the number twelve is not important to this study. *What is important is that we see that Jesus kept the number He would work with small enough so that He could have an intimate relationship with them.* Jesus devoted most of His ministry life to those twelve for the purpose of training them to disciple others. And it took Him three years to do the job.

In following Jesus' example, our first step in making disciples is also that of selection. As we become mature, active Christians, we are going to be evangelizing the unsaved and fellowshipping with many believers that need someone to look after them in the Lord and help them grow to become mature disciples. Since you are just one person, you cannot give all of those you come in contact with the personal attention they need. *Disciples cannot be mass produced. So you must choose a few.* You invite them to become your student and companion in the Lord for the purpose of teaching them, pouring your life into them and then sending them out to do the same for others.

God began to show me this need for selection while I was ministering to a group of people in Houston, Texas. Because God was moving in an exciting way in the meetings, the attendance grew. People were saved, baptized, touched by God's Spirit and began to witness to their friends and relatives. Then more would come and the cycle would repeat itself. It was exciting.

But something troubled me deeply. As time passed, I noticed that a certain number of the people began to drift away and were not as involved as they had been at the beginning. They were going back to the world and their old ways. I then realized that there were some who would go on with God and some who would not and that I needed to give my time and attention to those who would.

Making The Right Choice

How do you know whom to choose? Just as with Jesus, it is a matter of prayer, spiritual insight and observation. You only have so much time. You only have so much energy. You only have one life to give. As cold as this may sound, you simply cannot waste it on those who are not willing to follow, learn and imitate Christ in you.

The Bible gives us some guidance on the type of person to choose. Paul instructed Timothy, "And these things that you have heard from me among many witnesses, commit these to faithful men who will be able to teach others also" (2 Timothy 2:2 NKJ).

The guideline which Paul gives is *faithfulness.* We should look for faithful people. A faithful person is one who is reliable and trustworthy. From the standpoint of discipleship, this is a person whom you believe will receive what you are able to teach them and who, in turn, will teach others.

But of all the people you come into contact with, how can you tell which ones will be faithful. I believe a faithful person possesses certain identifiable characteristics which we are now going to discuss.

A. Teachable Spirit

The first characteristic of faithful persons is that they have a teachable spirit. We all know that we can't teach someone who is not open to instruction nor willing to learn. David expressed a teachable spirit when he cried out to God, "Search me, O God, and know my heart: try me, and know my thoughts: And see if there be any wicked way in me, and lead me in the way everlasting" (Psalms 139:23-24 KJV).

You can tell if a person has a teachable spirit by their willingness to receive instruction and correction.

B. Hunger for God

A person who has a hunger for God will make the necessary commitment to know Him better. *Those who only have a superficial interest will not be faithful.* Again, we turn to David as an example of one who hungered for God. David expressed his longing for God with these words, "O God, You are my God; Early will I seek You; My soul thirsts for You In a dry and thirsty land Where there is no water. So I have looked for You in the sanctuary, To see Your power and Your glory" (Psalms 63:1-2 NKJ).

Those who are hungry for God will spend regular time studying the Scriptures and be active and consistent in ministry opportunities provided to them by the local fellowship of which they are a part.

C. Submitted to Lordship of Christ

Another characteristic of faithful persons is that they are submitted to the Lordship of Christ. This simply means that they have recognized Jesus' claim on their life and they desire to know and do His will. *These are persons who seriously give first priority to the kingdom of God in their lives.* Paul spoke of this need with these words, "I beseech you therefore, brethren, by the mercies of God, that you present your bodies a living sacrifice, holy, acceptable to God, which is your reasonable service. And do not be conformed to this world, but be transformed by the renewing of your mind, that you may prove what is that good and acceptable and perfect will of God" (Romans 12:1-2 NKJ).

The person who is submitted to the Lordship of Christ earnestly seeks God's will for every area of his or her life and obeys it once it is revealed. *You can spot these people by their holy lives.*

D. Desire to be Used by God

The fourth quality of faithful people is that they desire to be used by God. They have a zeal for God and for the things that concern Him. God spoke to Isaiah about the need for someone to take us His cause. Isaiah responded with these words, ". . . Here am I! Send me" (Isaiah 6:8 NKJ).

A person who has a desire to be used by God will be available to God. You'll find them "hanging around", eager for an opportunity to serve God.

E. Concern for People

Finally, a faithful person is one who is concerned for people. *A person who does not have a genuine love and caring for others will not stick with it when the going gets rough and those they are ministering to let them down.* Paul demonstrated this concern in his own life and wrote the Christians at Philippi, "For God is my witness, how greatly I long for you all with the affection of Jesus" (Philippians 1:8 NKJ).

You can recognize persons who care for others by their desire to share the gospel and willingness to do works of lovingkindness.

Finding the Faithful

These are a few characteristics that can help you identify a faithful person. It's not likely that they will be in full bloom in the person, but you will certainly be able to recognize the seed in them. The person whose character demonstrates a growing measure of these qualities will be a faithful person. This is the type of person you want to choose to disciple.

Help as many people as you can, but select a small num-

ber that you can work with on a personal basis. Since Jesus could only handle twelve, I don't think we can do any better. So I suggest you limit your number to twelve. You may not be able to find twelve. If not, start with however many you can find whom you believe demonstrate the qualities of a faithful person. If it's just one person, begin with that one. If you are single, limit your choice to those of the same sex.

Issue the invitation to them with all boldness just as Jesus did with those He chose. Tell them what you have in mind and the commitment that is required. *Make sure they know exactly what will be expected of them.* Give them a week or two to count the cost. Then pray and wait for God to move on their heart. Based on Jesus' example and my own personal experiences in this type of ministry, it will take about three years to develop those you choose into mature disciples who are able to teach and reproduce Christ in others just as you have done for them.

As with Jesus, those you select will often disappoint you. This is to be expected and should not be overly discouraging. The end result of your effort will be a group of people who will carry on the ministry of Christ in you while you are with them and long after you have gone to be with Jesus.

2. Commit

The second step in the process of making a disciple is the *mutual commitment of lives.* During His ministry, Jesus did not totally neglect the crowds. He preached to them, fed them when they were hungry, healed them when they were sick, cast out demons when they were possessed and eventually gave His life for them. But He did not give His life to them.

As pointed out earlier, Jesus knew that the crowd, as a collective group, did not really understand nor desire to make the commitment to Him that He was offering. Because of this knowledge, Jesus was not going to make a commitment to them. *He ministered to the crowds, but His commitment was to His disciples.*

It's worth noting that Jesus spent more time with His

disciples than He did with everybody else all together. He called them to be with Him. We read in Mark 3:14, "Then He appointed twelve, that they might be *with Him . . ."* (NKJ).

Jesus and His disciples did things together. They prayed together. They ministered together. They had fun times together. They studied together. They witnessed together. As they did, a deep personal relationship began to form between them.

You see, the disciples were not just called by Jesus; they were called to Jesus. His interest was to share His life with them. They were not just to follow some teaching He gave, they were to follow Him. He not only showed them the way, He was the way. He not only taught them truth, He was the truth. He promised not only to give them life, He was the life (John 14:6).

Jesus was the very Word of God in the flesh (John 1:1,14). His purpose was not just to inform His disciples, but to form them into His own moral image. He was not so much interested in implementing His teachings as He was imparting His life. *The disciples were not just to know about Him, they were to be like Him.* The life of Jesus was not something that was only to be taught, it had to be caught. This could only happen by Jesus giving Himself to His disciples, who in turn, committed their lives to Him and each other. *The good shepherd doesn't hide from the sheep; he gives his life to them.*

This mutual commitment of lives is probably the most difficult step of the entire process of making disciples. The reason is obvious. You must give your life to others and live primarily for their spiritual and moral benefit until they no longer are dependent on you. Your life will be centered around them rather than your own personal interests. In fact, they become your interest.

When I selected those whom I thought would be faithful, it was a matter of much prayer. I knew I would be investing my life in them, and I did not want to fail. Peggy and I began to meet with a small group who had mutually agreed to commit their lives to us and each other. We spent more time with them than we did everybody else all together. We prayed together, studied together, played together, rejoiced and wept together, witnessed together, etc., and a deep personal relationship formed between us. Our lives were "rubbing off" on each other.

Imparting Life

When you become a Christian, the Word of God (Jesus) comes to live in your flesh by the Holy Spirit. You are not the Word of God, but He does live in you. *Your objective as a disciple maker is not only to teach those you have selected, but also to reproduce Christ in them. You yourself are the living Bible class from which those whom you have selected will, spiritually speaking, "catch Christ." The only way you can impart His life to them is by being with them.* This requires that you give your very life to them just as parents must give their life to their children until they are able to live mature lives on their own.

You must pray for them and with them. You must bear their burdens until they are able to bear them for themselves. You must counsel them until they know the mind of Christ. You love them until they know how to love. You give yourself to them until they learn how to give themselves to others. You pray, worship, study, minister, witness and fellowship together.

The apostle Paul often referred to this committed relationship that existed between him and those to whom he was ministering. He wrote to the Thessalonians, "So, affectionately longing for you, we were well-pleased to impart to you not only the gospel of God, but also our own lives, because you have become dear to us" (1 Thessalonians 2:8 NKJ).

He reminded Timothy of their relationship with these words, "But you have carefully followed my doctrine, manner of life . . ." (2 Timothy 3:10 NKJ).

He wrote to the Galatian Christians, "My little children, for whom I labor in birth again until Christ is formed in you" (Galatians 4:19 NKJ). Here Paul compares his relationship to the Galatians as a mother with child who endures the pains of pregnancy and labor as she gives birth to a fully formed baby.

Committing your life to those you have chosen to disciple is spiritual birthing and parenting. There will be many spiritual labor pains. You'll sometimes wonder if it's all worth the effort. But as every mother knows, the joys of seeing that fully formed baby more than offset the pain and sacrifice that are part of the birthing process. Likewise, the joys of helping another believer grow to maturity in Christ more than compensate for the heartaches and difficulties that can accompany that very special spiritual life-giving relationship.

3. Teach

The third step in this process is to teach those you are discipling about God and His ways. Jesus spent time with His disciples for the purpose of teaching them and imparting His life to them. *As we noted earlier, He taught them in two ways—by word and example.* Luke writes, ". . . of all that Jesus began to do and teach" (Acts 1:1 NKJ).

Jesus spent many long hours teaching His disciples from the Scriptures. Sometimes He taught them formally through a lecture such as the Sermon on the Mount. At other times, He taught them informally. If they didn't understand what Jesus was talking about, they had plenty of opportunities to ask Him because they were always together.

But just teaching them was not enough. It was important that the disciples see Jesus live out His teachings. Jesus' teaching method was to explain a spiritual or moral truth to the disciples, then demonstrate that truth in His life so they could see it being lived out in human flesh.

For example, Jesus taught the disciples how to pray, then He let them see Him pray. He taught them about healing, then He held a healing crusade. He taught them about deliverance, then He delivered people from evil spirits. He taught them about the moral character of God, then He lived out that character so they could witness it. He taught them about relationships, then He practiced what He preached. Since the disciples were constantly with Him, they were always in class listening to what Jesus said and then observing all that He did.

Helping Them Learn

The main reason we commit ourselves to others is to teach them to know God and walk with Him while imparting His life in us to them. We do this the same way Jesus did it. *We must spend many long hours with those we are discipling for the purpose of teaching them from the Scriptures. This means, of course, that we must know the Scriptures ourselves.* Sometimes we will teach them through a formal lecture such as at a Bible study. At other times, we will teach them informally as we develop a meaningful relationship together.

But just teaching them with words is not enough. We must practice what we preach so that those under our care can see the teaching being lived out in our flesh. The following poem by Edgar Guest relates to this. He said, *"I'd rather see a sermon, than hear one any day. I'd rather one would walk with me than merely tell the way."*

This poem describes how Jesus taught His disciples and how we should teach those whom He has given us. We need to teach them with words, both formally and informally, in order to give them information. Then we need to show them how these words are to be lived out in everyday life experiences. This is how people learn. This does not mean that we will be perfect in our example. But we must strive with all of God's help to live a blameless life. *Knowing that people are going to reproduce what they see in you is the greatest incentive for desiring to imitate Christ.*

The group Peggy and I worked with was a real challenge to teach because they came from vastly different backgrounds. I had to teach at a level they could all understand and relate to from their varied perspectives of life. Some who were more formally educated appreciated a lecture.

Others who had little formal education could learn more easily through a simple conversation over lunch. To some, Jesus was our "propitiation" while to others He was the "super-cool" Son of God. And I learned that a "ghetto blaster" was not a double barreled shotgun but a big radio that made lots of noise.

4. Assign

After Jesus taught His disciples and demonstrated His teaching through His life, He then gave them an opportunity to put the teachings into practice for themselves. *He gave them assignments to perform.* At first, these were simple tasks such as tending to the physical necessities that were part of the ministry. These were certainly not world-shaking responsibilities. But as the disciples proved faithful in the little matters, Jesus began to give them more important assignments. For example, he allowed them to baptize those who were responding to His message. (John 4:2).

As the disciples listened and observed, there finally came a time when Jesus felt it appropriate to allow them to participate more directly in His ministry. It was time for the disciples to put into practice what they had been learning from Jesus. They were to have *on-the-job training.* We read in Mark, "And He called the twelve to Him, and began to send them out two by two . . ." (Mark 6:7 NKJ).

Jesus called the twelve to Him. This was a planning session in which Jesus would explain their assignment in great detail. He told them where they were to go, what they were to say and what they were to do and not to do (Matthew 10:5-15). He then sent them out to do the task He had given them with instructions to report back to Him at a certain time. They would then share their experiences with Jesus and each other and learn how to relate them to practical areas of discipleship in their own lives.

Mark tells us, "Then the apostles gathered to Jesus and told Him all things, both what they had done and what they had taught. And He said to them, "Come aside by yourselves to a deserted place and rest a while." For there were many coming and going, and they did not even have time to eat. So they departed to a deserted place in the boat by themselves" (Mark 6:30-32 NKJ).

We learn from these verses that Jesus personally supervised the disciples' work. *He gave them an assignment, He held them accountable and He evaluated their progress.* As they became more effective, He gave them more frequent and important assignments. Jesus continued to train the disciples in this way until they were ready to minister on their own.

Practicing the Principles

In teaching those we are discipling, it's important to give them an opportunity to *try out* the teachings for themselves. At first, you give them simple tasks to get their feet wet. Then as they prove faithful and gain confidence, you give them more important responsibilities. You help them recognize their particular ministry function in the body of Christ and give them opportunities to develop their anointed abilities and spiritual gifts. You provide them with situations in which they can share their faith. You instruct them, correct them, praise them and point out lessons for them to learn from their experiences. You oversee their progress until they are ready to minister on their own independent of you.

It was such a joy for Peggy and I to see those we were ministering to grow to a place where they were ready and able to take on responsibilities themselves. At first, the steps were small. But as they proved themselves, their involvement and participation became more active and important. They took on larger roles. They were now doing the preaching, praying, singing, sharing, caring, etc. They were discovering their own abilities, gifts and ministries and were beginning to minister independent of me.

5. Send

Jesus' goal was to produce mature disciples who could share His words and His life with others without Him having to be there with them in the flesh. *His plan was to select a few faithful men, commit and impart His life to them, teach them, give them on-the-job training, and then send them out to do in the lives of others what He had done in their lives.* This was the way Jesus was going to build His church and establish the kingdom of God in the hearts of men and women who would receive His message and His life.

Jesus knew that there would come a time when He would no longer be with His disciples in His human body. He was going to die, be raised from the dead and ascend back to heaven. As that time drew near, Jesus prayed earnestly for His disciples. *He did not pray for the crowd. He prayed for His disciples and for those who would become His disciples.* One of His disciples, John, was so deeply moved by Jesus' prayer that he recorded it for us.

Jesus began His prayer by thanking His heavenly Father for the opportunity to make these initial disciples and for completing the work. He said, "I have glorified You on earth. I have finished the work which You have given Me to do" (John 17:4 NKJ).

Then He began to pray for His disciples. He said, "I pray for them. I do not pray for the world but for those who You have given Me, for they are Yours (verse 9 NKJ). As we read Jesus' prayer for His disciples, we find that He prayed that the Father would keep them from being overcome by Satan and sanctify them through His word so that their ministry might be successful.

Jesus then prayed for those who would come to Him through His disciples' ministry. He spoke these words, "I do not pray for these along, but also for those who will believe in Me through their word" (verse 20 NKJ). His prayer was that, through love, they would be in such perfect unity that the world would know who Jesus was and what He had come to do.

After Jesus was resurrected, He appeared to His disciples and said, ". . . As the Father has sent Me, I also send you" (John 20:21 NKJ). Later, just before He ascended back to heaven, He sent them into the world with these words,

". . . All authority has been given to Me in heaven and on earth. Go therefore and make disciples of all the nations, baptizing them in the name of the Father and of the Son and of the Holy Spirit, teaching them to observe all things that I have commanded you; and lo, I am with you always, even to the end of the age . . ." (Matthew 28:18-20 NKJ). Jesus then empowered them with the Holy Spirit so they could carry out this commission.

Letting Them Go

Our goal in making disciples is to develop mature Christian men and women who can pass on the Word of God and impart His life to others without us having to be there personally to help them. We want them to become independent of us and dependent on Jesus through the ministry of the Holy Spirit, as were the first disciples. *So there comes a point in time when we too should gently push our spiritual children out of the nest to stand on their own.* We thank God for giving them to us. We pray for them. We pray for those whom they will disciple. We send them out into the world. And we let them know that we will always be there if they need us, even to the end of our life.

I'm so grateful for those God has allowed me to help develop and bring to maturity in Christ. And yes, there came a point in time when I had to let them go to be their own men and women of God. At first Peggy and I experienced what all parents must face when their children leave home-the empty nest blues. We have gotten over that now, but we are always thrilled to hear from these very special loved ones and to see the image of Jesus in them. I don't know how Peggy feels, but it sure is lonely around here. I wonder if she would like to have more children?

Getting Started

If you have never had the joyous privilege of making disciples for our Lord Jesus Christ, I pray that you will start right now. It won't be easy. It will take a long time. There will be many disappointments and probably no human recognition. Additionally, it will cost you much of your life. But isn't that what being a Christian is all about—giving our lives to others? *You will find no greater satisfaction than that of investing your life in someone else for the purpose of imparting Christ's life to them.* The result will be an extension of your own ministry and life through others and lasting fruit from your labor.

I have written this book in love. And I know it has been straightforward, hardhitting and demanding in its call to unreserved commitment to the Lord Jesus Christ. I pray that you will now make that commitment and begin to lead others in doing so as well. But how do you get started?

You must first make an honest appraisal of your level of Christian commitment and maturity. Based on your appraisal, you either start your own discipleship group with a few faithful people who look to you for leadership, or you ask your spiritual leader to disciple you. Ideally, this should be done within the framework of the local church.

The ministry of discipleship takes place in small group settings under the leadership of the Holy Spirit working through the disciple maker. It's probably best done in the home. The group meeting should be informal and limited to twelve participants. It should meet once a week. The leader should give the participants daily Bible study assignments that will be discussed at the discipleship meeting. *These should be structured assignments designed to build knowledge, Christ-likeness and relationships among the participants.* It is difficult to find Bible study materials designed for this purpose. One organization that provides excellent material for this type of ministry is Lay Leadership Institute, 1267 Hicks Boulevard, Fairfield, Ohio 45014, (513) 829-1999. They can assist you in getting started.

The typical discipleship meeting will include praise and worship, discussion of weekly assignments, prayer, ministry of the Holy Spirit to and through each participant and fellowship. As the participants mature, they will bring others to Christ and begin their own discipleship meeting. In this way, the message and life of Jesus Christ will multiply and change the world in fulfillment of the Great Commission.

The organized church has tried to save the lost and win communities to Christ through revival meetings conducted by evangelists. This approach has not been successful and never will be. The reason is simple. The evangelist adds converts, but the population multiplies. People multiply at a much faster rate than the evangelist can add them to the church.

In order to keep up with the population growth, we must do more than just add converts. *We must make disciples.* Consider these facts. If an evangelist added 1,000 people to the church every night of the year, it would take him 10,000 years to win the whole world to Christ. However, if one disciple of Jesus was to win just one person each year and disciple that person to win one other person the following year and so forth, it would take only 32 years to win the whole world to Christ.

The following appendices will help you determine your own level of Christian maturity and provide you with guidance concerning the training necessary to lead others into a deeper relationship with Christ. Please study the material that is provided. Then share it with at least *one other person* whom you believe would respond to your spiritual leadership.

May God bless you and help you to become all that He wants you to be and do all that He wants you to do through Jesus Christ our Lord!

Chapter 6—How do We Make Disciples?

Review Exercise

1. List the five steps involved in making disciples.

    a.

    b.

    c.

    d.

    e.

2. List the five characteristics of a faithful person.

    a.

    b.

    c.

    d.

    e.

3. How can you apply this knowledge to your own life?

Appendix 1

Christian Growth Profile

We have learned in this book that Jesus calls us to be His disciples. Anyone who accepts Jesus as their Savior must also acknowledge Him as their Lord. We must follow Him, learn of Him and imitate Him. The Christian's objective is to grow into the image of Jesus Christ and learn how to lead others to do the same. This is a growth process in which the Christian must be taught by word and example.

This growth does not just happen automatically. It must be planned for with definite objectives in mind. In view of this, it is important to know where the individual Christian is in his or her growth and development. A *Christian Growth Profile* such as the one in this appendix can be very helpful. The purpose of the *Christian Growth Profile* is to provide a tool for identifying where people are in their walk with God. This is not a critical judgemental evaluation. It is simply a Godly observation of the believers life for the purpose of determining the type of training and development he or she needs.

The *Christian Growth Profile* is divided into the four phases through which believers progress in their growth and development. These are:

1. *New convert*
2. *Growing Christian*
3. *Maturing disciple*
4. *Leader*

The characteristics you would expect to see in the lives of believers in each phase of their development is listed. You can use this to help you determine how people are progressing in their walk with God. This will help you choose the type of training they need. Appendix Two discusses the training that is appropriate for each phase of the *Christian Growth Profile*.

When you lead people to Christ, you want to make sure they have a *genuine conversion experience.* One way to help you determine this is to compare the persons life with the characteristics of a new convert.

As you work with the new converts in personal follow-up, you expect to see them *grow* in their understanding of God and commitment to Christ and each other. You can check their progress by comparing their lives and actions to the characteristics of a growing Christian.

It is out of this group of growing Christians that you select a small group to *disciple* on a more intimate basis. As you work with the small group, you will be able to observe each persons life looking for the characteristics of a maturing disciple.

Finally, from the group of disciples will emerge *leaders.* These are mature disciples whom God is raising up as servant leaders to help others grow in their development just as you have helped them. Through these leaders, you will be reproducing Christ in others and multiplying disciples just as surely as if you were doing it personally yourself.

It should be clear that it takes time for believers to progress through the *four phases* of Christian maturity. The time involved will vary depending on the individual and his or her commitment to growth. A general time schedule which is considered normal for most believers is as follows:

1. *New convert* - 0 to 6 months
2. *Growing Christian* - 6 months to $2\frac{1}{2}$ years
3. *Maturing disciple* - $2\frac{1}{2}$ to 3 years
4. *Leader* - 3 years $(+)$

Although this may seem like a lot of time, we must remember that it took Jesus three years to transform and mold His twelve followers into usable disciples. It will take us no less. The teachings necessary to help believers grow through these four phases are explained in Appendix Two.

CHRISTIAN GROWTH PROFILE

New Convert	Growing Christian	Maturing Disciple	Leader
1. Clear profession of faith in Christ as personal Savior. 2. Willingness to submit to water baptism. 3. Desire to fellowship with other Christians. 4. Some change in life-style.	1. Desire to know God better. 2. Desire to be used by God. 3. Consistent in fellowship. 4. Consistent in Bible study. 5. Consistent in prayer. 6. Gives tithes and offerings. 7. Consistent in witnessing. 8. Not entangled with world. 9. Disciplined. 10. Diligent. 11. Faithful.	1. Agape love. 2. Bears fruit. 3. Obedient. 4. Submissive. 5. Servant. 6. Reproduces.	1. Spiritual authority. 2. Sure of calling and ministry. 3. Example in life. 4. Able to admonish and counsel others. 5. Ability to communicate and teach. 6. Self-motivated. 7. Able to make decisions. 8. Organizational skills.

- New convert - 0 to 6 months
- Growing Christian - 6 months to 2½ years
- Disciple - 2½ years to 3 years
- Leader - 3 years (+)

Appendix 2

Pathway To Christian Maturity

We have mentioned that the Christian's objective is to grow into the image of Jesus Christ and learn how to lead others to do the same. This Christian growth takes place as the believer is taught by word and example. Teaching by the Word of God informs believers. Teaching by example forms them into the image of Jesus Christ.

Teaching and molding the believer does not take place haphazardly. There are definite things that must be learned along the way in each phase of Christian development. These teachings should be planned and presented systematically in order to lay a firm foundation on which to build for the next phase. The teachings cover those subjects that are appropriate for believer's in each phase of their development.

The various teachings should be grouped and presented with certain training goals in mind. These are as follows.

1. *Training goal for new convert*
   • To confirm and assure genuineness of conversion experience.
2. *Training goal for growing Christian*
   • To establish and stabilize convert in the faith.
3. *Training goal for maturing disciple*
   • To produce maturity and fruitfulness in the believer's life.
4. *Training goal for leader*
   • To develop the ability to lead others in spiritual growth and commitment.

The chart in this appendix entitled *Pathway to Christian Maturity* provides a plan for teaching the believer systematically through the four phases of development. The chart shows subject matter, approximate number of lessons, teaching method and phase for which the teaching is appropriate. It provides for a balance between formal lecture and small home share group discipleship meetings.

The primary purpose of the lecture is to give out information. The purpose of the home share group meeting is to form Christ in the believer. This is accomplished as the participant performs daily Bible study assignments and begins to put what has been learned into practice through relationships in the small group setting.

This is a generalized plan that must be adapted to the specific needs of a local fellowship or study group. It is flexible enough for you to work out your own schedule of implementation according to you own particular objectives and circumstances. Thus the schedule may be expanded, compressed, or arranged in whatever way is desirable.

Get familiar with the *Pathway to Christian Maturity* chart. Then study each of the remaining appendices. They provide a teaching plan that meets the training and maturity requirements of the four phases of Christian growth. The plan includes the training goal, subject, number of sessions (in parenthesis), topics, reference material and study outlines. This is very valuable information so please review it carefully.

Reference material available from Sounds of the Trumpet, Inc. may be ordered by completing and mailing the Order Form which is provided on the last page of this book following the tape list.

PATHWAY TO CHRISTIAN MATURITY

Subject	Number of Sessions	Teaching Method	New Convert	Growing Christian	Maturing Disciple	Leader
Foundational Studies (overview)	12	Lecture	X			
* You Are Welcome	8	HSG	X			
Practical Studies	22	Lecture		X		
* First Things First	28	HSG		X		
Foundational Studies (in-depth)	64	Lecture		X		
* New Life Studies	9	HSG		X		
Discipleship	8	Lecture			X	
* Pathway to Discipleship	36	HSG			X	
* Fishers of Men	9	HSG			X	
Managing Your Life	4	Lecture				X
Helping Others	4	Lecture				X
* Ministry Principles	9	HSG				X

* Available from Lay Leadership Institute

HSG - Home Share Group

Appendix 3

Training The New Convert

A. Training Goal

To confirm and assure genuineness of conversion experience.

B. Subject

Foundational Studies (Overview)

C. Number of Sessions

1. Lecture—12
2. Home Share Group—8

D. Topics

1. Knowing the Bible (1)
2. Knowing God (1)
3. Knowing Jesus Christ (1)
4. Knowing the Holy Spirit (1)
5. Knowing Man (1)
6. Knowing the Enemy (1)
7. Living the Abundant Life (1)

8. Water Baptism (1)
9. Communion (1)
10. Nature of the Church (1)
11. The End Times (1)
12. Life After Death (1)

E. Reference Materials

1. Lecture

   Foundational Studies—1, Cassette Tape Series (Sounds of the Trumpet).

   Foundational Studies—2, Cassette Tape Series (Sounds of the Trumpet).

2. Home Share Group

   You are Welcome—An 8-lesson workbook written for the purpose of helping people to discover the gospel for themselves.

F. Bible Study Outlines

The following Bible Study Outlines are for the foundational studies.

KNOWING THE BIBLE

1. Authority of the Bible
   (2 Tim. 3:16)
2. Purpose of the Bible
   (2 Tim. 3:15-17)
3. Instruction to Study the Bible
   (Deut. 6:6-7;Josh. 1:8;2 Tim. 2:15)
4. Story of the Bible
   (Luke 24:25-27,44-47)
5. Teacher of the Bible
   (John 14:26;15:26;16:13)
6. Attitudes in Bible Study
   A. New Heart—Ezek. 36:26;1 Cor. 2:9–14
   B. Humble Heart—James 4:6
   C. Obedient Heart—Ps. 119:97–104
   D. Hungry Heart—Matt. 5:6
7. Benefits of Bible Study
   A. Strong Christian—1 Pet. 2:2
   B. Cleansed of Sin—John 15:3
   C. Bear Fruit—John 15:4–5
   D. How to Pray—John 15:7
   E. Guidance—Ps. 119:105

KNOWING GOD

1. God's Witness to His Existence
    A. Creation—Ps. 19:1
    B. Instinct—Rom. 1:18-19;2:14-15
    C. Bible—2 Tim. 3:16
    D. Jesus Christ—John 14:8-9
2. God's Personality
    A. Self-Existing—Ex. 3:13-14
    B. Spirit—John 4:24
    C. Personal—Prov. 9:10
    D. Unity—Deut. 6:4
    E. Trinity—Matt. 28:19
3. God's Majestic Attributes
    A. Sovereign—Ps. 47:6-8
    B. All Power—Rev. 19:6
    C. All Knowledge—1 John 3:20
    D. Everywhere Present—Jer. 23:23-24
    E. Never Changes—Mal. 3:6
4. God's Moral Attributes
    A. Holy—Rev. 15:4
    B. Love—1 John 4:7-8
    C. Just—Deut. 32:4
    D. Good—Ps. 34:8

KNOWING JESUS CHRIST

1. His Deity
   (Is. 9:6;Mic. 5:2;John 1:1;20:28)
2. His Humanity
   (John 1:14;Gal. 4:4;Heb. 2:14-18)
3. His Substitutionary Death
   (Rom. 3:20-25;6:23;10:9-10;2 Cor. 5:21)
4. His Resurrection
   (Matt. 16:21;28:1-6;John 20:11-17)
5. His Exaltation
   (Acts 1:9-11;2:30;Eph. 1:20-23;Rev. 1:10-18)
6. His Return
   (John 14:1-3;1 Thess. 4:13-17;Rev. 19:11-16)
7. His Everlasting Rule
   (Is. 9:7;Ps. 2)

Study Outline Number 4
KNOWING THE HOLY SPIRIT

1. His Personality
   (John 14:16-17,26;16:7-15)
   A. He Reproves (Convicts)—John 16:8
   B. He Teaches—John 14:26;16:13-15
   C. He Speaks—1 Tim. 4:1
   D. He Leads—Rom. 8:14
   E. He Bears Witness—Rom. 8:16
   F. He Appoints—Acts 13:2
   G. He is Jealous—James 4:5
2. His Work in Regeneration
   (John 3:1-7;Titus 3:5)
3. His Indwelling
   (John 4:13-14;7:37-39;14:17)
4. His Sealing
   (Is. 49:16;2 Cor. 1:22;Eph. 1:13;4:30)
5. His Filling
   (Eph. 5:18;Acts 1:8;2:4;4:8,31)
6. Offenses Against
   A. Blaspheming—Matt. 12:31–32
   B. Insulting—Heb. 10:29
   C. Resisting—Acts 7:51
   D. Lying to—Acts 5:3-4
   E. Grieving—Eph. 4:30-31
   F. Quenching—1 Thess. 5:19

KNOWING MAN

1. Created in God's Image
   (Gen. 1:26-27;1 Thess. 5:23-24)
2. Man's Original Sin
   (Gen. 2:15-17;3:1-24)
3. Sin Nature Inherited
   (Rom. 5:12,19;Mark 7:14-23;Jer. 17:9;Gen. 8:21)
4. Sin Separates Man from God
   (Rom. 3:10-12;John 3:16-20;Is. 59:1-2)
5. Natural Man Cannot Know God
   (1 Cor. 2:9-14)
6. Man Cannot Earn His Way Back to God
   (Is. 64:6;Eph. 2:8-9;Titus 3:5-7)
7. Man Reconciled to God
   (1 Tim. 2:5;John 14:6;Gal. 3:26)

KNOWING THE ENEMY

1. Satan—the Real Enemy
   (Eph. 6:10-12)
2. Satan's Origin and Fall
   (Ezek. 28:12-19;Is. 14:10-16)
3. Satan's Demonic Army
   (Jude 6;2 Pet. 2:4;Rev. 12:4,9)
4. Satan's Present Position
   (2 Cor. 4:4;Eph. 2:2;John 12:31;14:30;16:11;1 John 5:18-19)
5. Satan's Goal
   (Is. 14:14;Rev. 9:20-21)
6. Satan's Character
   A. Sifts—Luke 22:31
   B. Devours—1 Pet. 5:8
   C. Lies and Murders—John 8:44
   D. Crafty—Eph. 6:11
   E. Angel of Light—2 Cor. 11:4,13-15
   F. Deceiver—Rev. 12:9
   G. Accuses (Condemns)—Rev. 12:10
   H. Blinds—2 Cor. 4:4
   I. Snatches—Matt. 13:19
   J. Tempts—Matt. 4:3
7. Satan's Defeat and Destiny
   (Col. 2:15;Heb. 2:14;Matt. 25:41;Rev. 20:2,10)

Study Outline Number 7

LIVING THE ABUNDANT CHRISTIAN LIFE

1. Knowing Your Dominion
   A. Sin—Rom. 6:14
   B. Death—Rom. 8:11
   C. Satan—1 John 4:4
2. Identifying with Christ
   A. Crucified—Rom. 6:6;Gal. 2:20
   B. Buried—Rom. 6:3-4
   C. Raised—Rom. 6:8-13
   D. Seated—Eph. 2:4-6
3. Appropriating His Lordship
   (Rom. 12:1-2;John 12:24-26)
4. Walking in the Spirit
   (Eph. 5:18;Gal. 5:16-25)
5. Wearing the Armor
   (Eph. 6:10-18)

WATER BAPTISM

1. Meaning of Water Baptism
   A. An Outward Act
   B. Picturing an Inward Spiritual Change
   C. In Our Position Before God
      (Rom. 6:3-5;Gal. 3:27-28;1 Cor. 12:13)
2. Purpose of Water Baptism
   A. A Public Testimony
   B. To New Life in Christ
      (2 Cor. 5:17)
3. Why Should We be Baptised
   (Matt. 28:19)
4. Who Should be Baptised
   (Mark 1:4-5;16:15-16;Acts 2:38-41;8:36-37;16:14-15,31-34)
5. How are We Baptised
   (Matt. 3:16;Mark 1:9-10;John 3:23;Acts 8:38-39)

COMMUNION

1. Meaning of Communion
   A. An Outward Act
   B. Testifying to
   C. An Inward Spiritual Reality
      (Jer. 31:31-34;Ezek. 11:19-20;36:26-27;John 6:48-58,63)
2. Purpose of Communion
   A. Reminder of Christ's Death and Resurrection
   B. Reminder of Our Spiritual Union with Christ and Each Other
      (1 Cor. 10:16-17)
3. Why We Should Take Communion
   (Matt. 26:26-28;Mark 14:22-24;Luke 22:19-20)
4. Who Should Take Communion
   (Ex. 12:43-45,48;Acts 2:41-42;20:7)
5. Attitude Toward Communion
   (Lev. 7:20;1 Cor. 11:23-30)

THE NATURE OF THE CHURCH

1. What is the Church?
   (Matt. 16:13-18)
2. The Purpose of the Church
   (Acts 15:14;Eph. 3:10,21)
3. The Nature of the Church
   A. The Body of Christ
      (1 Cor. 12:12-27;Eph. 1:22-23;Col. 1:18)
   B. The Bride of Christ
      (2 Cor. 11:2;Eph. 5:23-32;Rev. 21:7-9)
   C. The Temple of God
      (Eph. 2:20-22;1 Cor. 3:16;6:16,19-20)
   D. The Priesthood of God
      (1 Pet. 2:5-9;Rev. 5:9-10;20:6)
   E. The Flock of God
      (John 10:1-16,27-28;21:15-17;Acts 20:28)
   F. The Branches
      (John 15:1-16;Gal. 5:22-25)

THE END TIMES

1. Signs of His Coming
   (Matt. 24:2 Pet. 3:3-6;2 Tim. 3:1-5;4:1-4)
2. Judgement of Christians
   (Rom. 14:10-12;1 Cor. 3:1-15;9:27;4:5;2 Cor. 5:10)
3. Seven-Year Tribulation
   (Deut. 4:30;Dan. 12:1;Matt. 24;Rev. 6-18)
4. Second Coming of Christ
   (Rev. 19:11-16)
5. The Millennium
   (Rev. 20:1-10)
6. Great White Throne Judgement
   (Rev. 20:11-15)
7. New Heaven and New Earth
   (Rev. 21-22)

Study Outline Number 12

LIFE AFTER DEATH

1. We Only Live Once
   (Heb. 9:27)
2. The Dead Before the Resurrection of Jesus
   A. Sheol
   B. Hades—Luke 16:19-31
3. What Jesus Did
   A. His Body in the Grave
      (Matt. 27:57-60)
   B. His Spirit and Soul in Torments
      (Ps. 16:10;88:6;Acts 2:30-31;13:35)
   C. His Spirit and Soul in Paradise
      (Ps. 68:18;Eph.4:8-10;1 Pet. 3:18-19;4:6)
   D. His Body, Spirit and Soul in Heaven
      (John 20:17;Acts 2:30-38;1 Pet. 3:22;Eph. 1:20-22)
4. The Dead After the Resurrection of Jesus
   A. Unbelievers
   B. Believers—(2 Cor. 12:1-4;5:8;Phil.1:23)
5. Resurrection of the Body
   A. All will be Resurrected—(John 5:22-29)
   B. Resurrection to Life—(1 Thess. 4:13-18;1 Cor. 15:51-58)
   C. Resurrection to Death—(Rev. 20:11-15;Matt. 10:15;11:22-24)
6. Hell
   (Matt. 10:28:Luke 12:4-5)
7. New Heaven and New Earth
   (Is. 65:17;Matt. 24:35;2 Pet. 3:7-14;Rev. 21-22)

Appendix 4

Training the Growing Christian

A. Training Goal

To establish and stablize convert in the faith.

B. Subject

Practical Studies

Foundational Studies (In-Depth)

C. Number of Sessions

1. Lecture
   A. Practical Studies—22
   B. Foundational Studies—64
2. Home Share Group
   A. *First Things First*—28
   B. *New Life Studies*—9

D. Topics

1. Practical Studies
   A. Living by Faith (1)
   B. Guidance (2)

  C. Prayer (2)
  D. Fasting (2)
  E. Meditation (1)
  F. Stewardship (2)
  G. Handling Trials (2)
  H. Sharing Your Faith (2)
  I. Worship and Priase (2)
  J. Health and Healing (2)
  K. Family Life (4)
 2. Foundational Studies (In-Depth)
  A. The Bible (14)
  B. Knowing God (14)
  C. The Blood Covenant (6)
  D. Life in the Spirit (6)
  E. The Church (8)
  F. Spiritual Warfare (8)
  G. End Times (8)

E. Reference Materials

 1. Lecture
  A. Practical Studies
   Practical Studies—1, Cassette Tape Series (Sounds of the Trumpet).
   Practical Studies—2, Cassette Tape Series (Sounds of the Trumpet).
   Faith and Healing, Cassette Tape Series (Sounds of the Trumpet).
   Christian Family, Cassette Tape Series (Sounds of the Trumpet).
  B. Foundational Studies
   Richard Booker, *Come and Dine* (Sounds of the Trumpet).
   Richard Booker, *Intimacy with God* (Sounds of the Trumpet).
   Richard Booker, *The Miracle of the Scarlet Thread* (Sounds of the Trumpet).
   Abundant Life Series, Cassette Tape Series (Sounds of the Trumpet).
   Richard Booker, *Seated in Heavenly Places*

(Sounds of the Trumpet).

The Church Series, Cassette Tape Series (Sounds of the Trumpet).

End Times Series, Cassette Tape Series (Sounds of the Trumpet).

Richard Booker, *Blow the Trumpet in Zion* (Sounds of the Trumpet).

2. Home Share Group
   A. *First Things First*— A 28-lesson workbook written for the purpose of helping newer Christians grow in their life with Christ.
   B. *New Life Studies*—A 9-lesson workbook that covers the essential foundational truths of the Christian faith.

F. Bible Study Outlines

The following Bible Study Outlines are for the practical and foundational studies. If you desire comprehensive Bible study materials on these subjects, you may order reference materials indicated from Sounds of the Trumpet by using the Order Form in the back of this book.

LIVING BY FAITH

1. Put God First in Everything
   (Matt. 6:24-34)
2. Give Your Burdens to God
   (1 Pet. 5:7;Matt. 10:29-31)
3. Pray with Thanksgiving
   (Phil. 4:6;1 Thess. 5:17)
4. Rejoice in the Lord
   (Phil. 4:4;1 Thess. 5:16)
5. Praise God Above All Things
   (Eph. 5:20;Acts 16:25)
6. Results of Living by Faith
   (Phil. 4:7;Is. 26:3-4;John 14:27; 16:33)

DIVINE GUIDANCE

1. God Wants to Guide You
   (Prov. 3:5-7)
2. Guidance From the Bible
   (Ps. 119:105)
3. Guidance from the Holy Spirit
   (John 16:13;Rom. 8:14)
4. Guidance Through Providence
   (Gen. 45:8;50:20)
5. Testing Guidance
   A. There are Three Spirits
      1. Holy Spirit—John 14:26
      2. Evil Spirits—Matt. 16:23
      3. Human Spirit—Rom. 8:16
   B. Peace or Confusion?
      (Col. 3:15)
   C. Agreement with Bible
      (1 Cor. 14:29-33)
   D. Share with Mature Christians
      (Prov. 11:14)
   E. Consider the Source of Guidance
      (Matt. 7:15-23)
   F. Consider the Spirit of Guidance
      (Gal. 6:1)

PRAYER

1. What is Prayer?
   Prayer is communicating with God and is His normally appointed means for working out His will and purposes for creation.
   (Jer. 33:3;1 Tim. 2:8)
2. The Purpose of Prayer
   The purpose of prayer is to glorify God and bring His will from heaven to earth.
   (John 14:13-14)
3. The Pattern of Prayer
   A. Worship—Giving glory to God for who He is in His perfections (1 Chr. 16:29)
   B. Praise—Giving glory to God for what He does. (Ps. 86:12)
   C. Confession—Agreeing with God concerning our sins. (Ps. 32:5;51:1-3)
   D. Intercession—Expressing concern for the needs of others. (1 Tim. 2:1)
   E. Petition—Expressing concern for your own needs. (Phil. 4:6)
4. Hindrances to Answered Prayer
   A. Wrong Motives—James 4:3
   B. Sin—Is. 59:1-2; Ps. 66:18
   C. Unforgiveness—Mark 11:25-26
   D. Marital Difficulties—1 Pet. 3:1-7
   E. Satanic Resistance—Dan. 10:12-14
   F. Unbelief—Mark 11:22-24;James 1:6-8;John 15:7
   G. Disobedience—1 John 3:22;Ps. 37:4-5
   H. Praying against God's will or character—1 John 5:14-15;John 14:13-14;16:23
5. Persistence in Prayer
   (Luke 11:5-10;18:1-8)

FASTING

1. The Meaning of Fasting
   To abstain from food or drink for religious purposes.
2. The Purpose of Fasting
   To concentrate attention on moral and spiritual concerns as a higher priority than fleshly appetites. It necessarily involves self-denial.
3. The Biblical Practice
   A. Mourning Over Sin—Lev. 16:29-31;Ps. 35:13;69:10 Joel 2:12-13;Jon. 3:1-5
   B. Intercession—Esth. 4:16;Deut. 9:18
   C. Seeking God's Assistance—Ezra 8:21-23
   D. Times of Crisis—2 Chr. 20:3;Esth. 4:3
   E. Grieving for God's Glory—Neh. 1:4;Ezra 10:6
   F. Personal Grief—1 Sam. 1:7;2 Sam. 12:16
   G. Fighting Temptation—Matt. 4:1-4
   H. Conducting Spiritual Warfare—Mat. 17:14-21
   I. Seeking Guidance—Acts 13:2-3
   J. For Leaders—Acts 14:23
   K. Mark of Sincerity—2 Cor. 6:4-5;11:23-27
   L. As a Life-Style—Luke 2:36-37
4. The Biblical Acknowledgement
   (Matt. 6:16-18;Mark 2:18-20;1 Cor. 7:5)
5. Degrees of Fasting
   A. Normal Fast (No Food)
   B. Partial Fast (Limited Intake)—Dan. 1:8,12;10:2-3
   C. Extreme Fast (No Food or Drink)—Ex. 34:28;1 Kin. 19:8
6. Types of Fast
   A. Private—Matt. 6:16-18
   B. Public—Judg. 20:26;Neh. 9:1-3;Joel 1:14;2:15-18

MEDITATION

1. The Meaning of Meditation
   Giving careful consideration and continuous thought to a specific Scripture.
2. The Biblical Instruction
   (Josh. 1:8;Ps. 1:1-3)
3. The Purpose of Meditation
   (Matt. 4:4;Col. 3:16; Ps. 119:11;John 15:7)
4. The Meditation Process
   A. Rumination
   B. Digesting God's Word
5. Steps to Meaningful Meditation
   A. Memorize
   B. Visualize
   C. Emphasize
   D. Personalize

STEWARDSHIP

1. God is the Owner, Man is the Steward
   A. God Owns Everything
      (1 Chr. 29:10-16)
   B. God has Special claim on Christians
      (1 Cor. 6:19-20)
2. Christian Stewardship
   A. Wisdom
      (Luke 16:1-13)
   B. Faithfulness
      (1 Cor. 4:1-2)
3. Giving in the Old Testament
   A. Giving the Tithe
      (Mal. 3:7-12)
   B. Giving Offerings
      (Ex. 35:5-9)
4. Giving in the New Testament
   A. Grace Not Law
      (Rom. 6:14;13:8-10)
   B. Principles of Christian Giving
      (2 Cor. 8-9)

HANDLING TRIALS

1. The Fact of Trials
   (Job 14:1; John 16:33)
2. The Purpose of Trials
   A. Test of Obedience
      (Deut. 8:2;Matt. 26:36-46)
   B. Develop Dependence On God
      (2 Cor. 12:9-10)
   C. Spiritual Growth
      (John 15:1-2;Rom. 5:3;James 1:2-4)
   D. Spiritual Discipline
      (Deut. 8:5;Heb. 12:5-11)
   E. Purifying
      (1 Pet. 1:6-9;Mal. 3:3;Job 23:8-10;42:5)
3. Responding to Trials
   A. Realize that God is in Charge
      (Is. 46:8-10;Job 34:21;Prov. 15:3;Gen. 45:7-8;50:20)
   B. Give God Your Burden
      (Ps. 50:15;1 Pet. 5:7)
   C. Rejoice in the Lord
      (1 Pet. 4:12-13;Hab. 3:17-19)
   D. Give God Praise
      (1 Pet. 4:14-19;1 Thess. 5:18)
   E. Meditate on God's Word
      (Ps. 119:92-93)
4. Rest in God
   (Rom. 8:28-29;1 Cor. 10:13;Ps. 34:19)

SHARING YOUR FAITH

1. The Great Commission
   (Matt. 28:18-20;Acts 1:8)
2. The Gospel Message
   A. All are Sinners—Rom. 3:23
   B. Result of Sin is Death—Rom. 6:23
   C. Man Cannot Save Himself—Eph. 2:8-9
   D. Christ Died to Save Us—Rom. 5:8-9
3. How to Receive Christ
   A. Believe—Acts 16:30-31
   B. Repent—Luke 5:32;13:3,5
   C. Ask—Rev. 3:20
   D. Confess—Rom. 10:9-13
4. Personal Testimony
   (Matt. 10:32-33)
5. How to Witness
   A. Pray—1 Tim. 2:1-4;John 17:15-21
   B. Be an Example—Acts 1:1
   C. Meet People at Their Point of Need—John 6:1-5,11-14,31-35
   D. Minister at Their Level—John 4:7-15
   E. Give Personal Testimony—1 Pet. 3:15;Eph. 6:19-20
   F. Focus on Jesus—John 12:32
      1. The Person of Jesus
         (2 Cor. 5:19;Col. 1:15;2:9)
      2. The Work of Jesus
         (Rom. 5:8-10;2 Cor. 5:18-21;Col. 1:20-22)
      3. The Necessity of Jesus
         (John 14:6;Acts 4:12;1 Tim. 2:5)

WORSHIP

1. The Meaning of Worship
   Giving glory to God for who He is (1 Chr. 16:29).
2. The Purpose of Worship
   To exalt God by showing Him honor and respect for His greatness (majesty) and moral perfections.
   Worship is expressed in adoration to God and service and sacrifice for God (2 king. 17:35-36).
   A. Adoration—2 Chr. 7:1-3;29:27-30;Ps. 95:6
   B. Service—Ps. 100:2;1 Thess. 1:9
   C. Sacrifice—2 Sam. 24:24;Ps. 96:8-9;Rom. 12:1-2
3. Reason for Worship
   God is worthy to be worshiped—Rev. 4:11;5:12
4. Instruction to Worship
   (Ps. 86:8-9;Matt. 4:10)
5. The Means and Place of Worship
   A. The Means—John 4:20-24;Phil. 3:3-4
   B. The Place—Rom. 8:15-17;Gal. 4:4-6
6. Expressions of Worship
   A. Prayer
   B. Scripture Reading
   C. Ministry of the Word
   D. Baptism and Communion
   E. Quiet Meditation
   F. Singing and Playing of Instruments
   G. Giving Ourselves and Finances in Service and Works of Lovingkindness

PRAISE

1. The Meaning of Praise
   Giving glory to God for what He does (Ps. 50:23;86:12).
2. The Purpose of Praise
   To exalt God by showing Him honor and respect for His mighty deeds and works of lovingkindness (Ps. 9:1-2;92:1-5;118:24;150:2).
3. The Reason for Praise
   God is worthy to by praised—Ps. 118:3;Rev. 4:11;5:12
4. Instruction to Praise
   (Ps. 100:4;1 Pet. 2:9;Rev. 19:5)
5. The Pattern of Praise
   A. With Song—Ps. 66:1;40:3;Eph. 5:19
   B. With Musical Instruments—Ps. 33:1-3;150:3-6
   C. With the Body—Ps. 84:2
      1. Mouth—Ps. 71:8;98:4-6;109:30
      2. Hands—Ps. 47:1,6-7;63:3-4;134:2
      3. Bowing and Kneeling—Ps. 95:6
      4. Standing—Ps. 134:1-2;135:1-3
      5. Dancing—2 Sam. 6:14;Ps. 149:1-3;150:4
6. The Order of Praise
   (1 Cor. 14:40)
7. The Time of Praise
   A. Good Times—Ps. 107:8-9,31-32
   B. Bad Times—Heb. 13:5;Eph. 5:20;Acts 16:25
   C. All Times—Ps. 34:1-4;104:33-35

HEALTH AND HEALING

1. Walking in Divine Health
   (Ex. 15:26;Prov. 3:7-8;4:20-22;Is. 53:4-5;1 Pet. 2:24;
   James 5:14-18)
2. Scriptural Faith for Healing
   (Matt. 17:14-20;Mark 11:22-24;Rom. 10:17;Heb. 12:2)
3. Barriers to Healing
   A. Sin and Sins
      (Gen. 3:16-19;2 Kin. 13:14;Rom. 8:18-23;2 Tim.
      4:20)
   B. Satanic Oppression
      (Job 2:1-10)
   C. Presumption
      (Ps. 127:2;Matt. 6:25-34;Phil. 2:25-30)
   D. Divine Judgement
      (Acts 13:6-11;Ps. 119:71;Rev. 16)

FAMILY LIFE

1. God's Purpose for Family
   A. Why God Made Us
      (Rev. 4:11)
   B. Marriage a Divine Ordinance
      (Mal. 2:15;Matt. 19:6;Mark 10:6-9)
   C. The First Family
      (Gen. 2:18-25)
   D. Family Life Temptation
      (Gen. 3)
   E. Family Life Restored
      (John 17)
2. The Husband's Role
   (1 Cor. 11:3;Eph. 5:21-6:4;1 Pet. 3:7)
3. The Wife's Role
   (Prov. 31;Eph. 5:22-24,33;1 Pet. 3:1-4)
4. Parent and Children Relationships
   (Eph. 6:1-4;Prov. 22:6;2 Tim. 3:15;Prov.
   22:15;23:14;24:12;29:15-19)

Study Outline Number 25

The Bible

1. What Makes the Bible Different?
   A. Title, Subject and Author
   B. Continuity
   C. Reliably Preserved
   D. Prophecies
   E. Changed Lives
2. How the Bible came Together
   A. The Ancient Test
   B. The Old Testament
   C. The Silent Years
   D. The New Testament
3. Old Testament Survey—1
   A. The Law
   B. History
   C. Poetry
4. Old Testament Survey—2
   A. Major Prophets
   B. Minor Prophets
5. New Testament Survey—1
   A. Gospels
   B. Church History
   C. Paul's Epistles
6. New Testament Survey—2
   A. General Epistles
   B. Prophecy
7. How We Got Our English Bible
   A. The Original Manuscripts
   B. Ancient Copies, Translations, Church Fathers
   C. The English Translations
8. How to Get into the Bible
   A. Keys to Effective Bible Study
   B. Blessings of Bible Study
   C. Attitudes in Bible Study

9. How to Read the Bible
   A. Begin at the Beginning
   B. Read in Easy Language Version
   C. Read Everyday
   D. Read at Regular Time
   E. Read at Regular Place
   F. Mark as you Read
10. How to Meditate
    A. Memorize
    B. Visualize
    C. Emphasize
    D. Personalize
11. How to Study a Bible Book
    A. Survey
    B. Analysis
    C. Summary
12. How to Study a Bible Topic
    A. Select Topic
    B. Look up References
    C. Arrange Verses
    D. Choose Examples
    E. Develop Outline
13. How to Understand the Bible
    A. Literal Sense
    B. Scripture with Scripture
    C. In Context
    D. Historically
    E. Correct Word Meanings
14. Basic Bible Study Aids
    A. Good Bible
    B. Study Notebook
    C. Concordance
    D. Bible Dictionary
    E. Bible Atlas
    F. One Volume Commentary

KNOWING GOD

1. Overview
2. Knowing God
   A. Creation—Ps. 19:1;Rom. 1:20
   B. Instinct—Rom. 1:18-19;2:12-15
   C. The Bible—2 Tim. 3:16
   D. Jesus Christ—John 14:8-9
3. God is Self-Existing
   A. Definition
   B. Eternal—Ps. 90:1-2;1 Tim. 1:7
   C. Infinite—1 Kin. 8:27;Jer. 23:24
4. God is Personal Spirit
   A. God is Personal—John 4:19-26
   B. God is Spirit—Prov. 9:10
5. God is Three in One
   A. God is a Unity—Deut. 6:4
   B. God is a Trinity—Matt. 28:19
6. God is Sovereign—Ps. 47:6-8
   A. Definition
   B. Nature—Ps. 135:5-6
   C. Individuals—Prov. 16:9
   D. Decree—Is. 46:8-10
   E. Flow of History—Ps. 22:28
7. God is All Power—Rev. 19:6
   A. Definition
   B. Creation—Heb. 11:3
   C. Becoming Man—Luke 1:30-37
   D. Life and Death—John 10:17-18
   E. Saving us from Sin—Matt. 19:23-26
   F. Keeping us from Sin—John 10:27-30
8. God is All Knowledge—1 John 3:20
   A. Definition
   B. God Knows Himself—Ex. 3:13-14
   C. God Knows What He is Doing—Eph. 1:4

     D. God Knows the Flow of History—Is. 46:9-10

     E. God Knows His Creatures—Ps. 139:1-5

9. God is Everywhere Present—Jer. 23:23-24

     A. Definition

     B. Jacob—Gen. 28:15-16

     C. Joshua—Deut. 31:1-8

     D. Disciples—Matt. 28:18-20

10. God is Unchanging—Mal. 3:6

     A. Definition

     B. God Himself Never Changes—James 1:17

     C. God's Decree Never Changes—Is. 46:9-10

     D. God's Word Never Changes—Ps. 119:89

11. God is Holy—Rev. 15:4

     A. Definition

     B. Glorious in Holiness—Ex. 15:11

     C. Works and Ways are Holy—Ps. 145:17

     D. Character is Holy—Hab. 1:13

     E. Holiness in His People—1 Pet. 1:14-16

12. God is Love—1 John 4:7-8

     A. Definition

     B. God's Love is Holy—1 John 1:5

     C. God's Love is Eternal—Jer. 31:3

     D. God's Love is Infinite—Rom. 8:35-39

     E. God's Love is Uncaused—1 John 4:9-10

     F. God's Love in His People—John 13:34-35

13. God is Just—Deut. 32:4

     A. Definition

     B. God's Ways are Just—Ps. 145:17

     C. God's Laws are Just—Ps. 19:7-8

     D. God's Judgement is Just—Ps. 119:137

     E. God's Wrath is Just—Num. 14:16

     F. God's Justice in His People—1 John 2:29

14. God is Good—Ps. 34:8

     A. Definition

     B. Creation—Gen. 1:31

     C. Dealings with Man—Ex. 33:19

     D. God's Goodness in Jesus Christ—Acts 10:38

     E. God's Goodness in His People—Matt. 5:16

THE BLOOD COVENANT

1. The Blood Covenant
   (1 Sam. 18:1-9)
2. What was it Abraham Believed?
   (Gen. 15)
3. The Tabernacle
   (Ex. 25-27;35-38)
4. The Sacrifices
   (Lev. 1-7)
5. The High Priest
   (Lev. 16)
6. The Passover
   (Ex. 12:1-14)

LIFE IN THE SPIRIT

1. Knowing Your Dominion
   A. Sin—Rom. 6:14
   B. Death—Rom. 8:11
   C. Satan—1 John 4:4
2. Identifying with Christ
   A. Crucified—Rom. 6:6;Gal. 2:20
   B. Buried—Rom. 6:3-4
   C. Raised—Rom. 6:8-13
   D. Seated—Eph. 2:4-6
3. Appropriating His Lordship
   (Rom. 12:1-2;John 12:24-26)
4. Walking in the Spirit—1
   (Eph. 5:18;Gal. 5:16-25)
5. Walking in the Spirit—2
   (Eph. 5:18;Gal. 5:16-25)
6. Ministering in the Spirit—1
   (Luke 4:18-21)
7. Ministering in the Spirit—2
   (Luke 4:18-21)
8. Wearing the Armor
   (Eph. 6:10-18)

THE CHURCH

1. Nature of the Church
   (Matt. 16:13-18;Acts 15:14;Eph. 3:10,21)
2. The Body of Christ
   (1 Cor. 12:12-27;Eph. 1:22-23;Col. 1:18)
3. Gifts of the Spirit—1
   (1 Cor. 12-14)
4. Gifts of the Spirit—2
   (1 Cor. 12-14)
5. Gifts of the Spirit—3
   (1 Cor. 12-14)
6. Equipping the Saints
   (Eph. 4:11-16)
7. Work of the Ministry
   (Luke 4:18-21)
8. Building up the Body
   (Rom. 12:3-10)

SPIRITUAL WARFARE

1. Background Information
   A. Satan—the Real Enemy
      (Eph. 6:10-12)
   B. Satan's Origin and Fall
      (Ezek. 28:12-19;Is. 14:10-16)
   C. Satan's Demonic Army
      (Jude 6;2 Pet. 2:4;Rev. 12:4,9)
   D. Satan's Present Position
      (2 Cor. 4:4;Eph. 2:2;John 12:31;14:30;16:11;1 John 5:18-19)
   E. Satan's Goal
      (Is. 14:14;Rev. 9:20-21)
   F. Satan's Defeat and Destiny
      (Col. 2:15;Heb. 2:14;Matt. 25:41;Rev. 20:2,10)
2. Satan's Character
   A. Sifts—Luke 22:31
   B. Devours—1 Pet. 5:8
   C. Lies and Murders—John 8:44
   D. Crafty—Eph. 6:11
   E. Angel of Light—2 Cor. 11:4,13-15
   F. Deceiver—Rev. 12:9
   G. Accuses (Condemns)—Rev. 12:10
   H. Blinds—2 Cor. 4:4
   I. Snatches—Matt. 13:9
   J. Tempts—1 John 3:8
3. Christian Armor
   A. Belt of Truth
      (Eph. 6:13-14;John 14:6)
   B. Breastplate of Righteousness
      (Eph. 6:14;1 John 2:1)
   C. Shoes of Peace
      (Eph. 6:15;Eph. 2:14)

D. Shield of Faith
   (Eph. 6:16;Heb. 12:2)
E. Helmet of Salvation
   (Eph. 6:17;1 Tim. 1:1)
F. Sword of Spirit
   (Eph. 6:17;John 1:1-3,14)

Study Outline Number 31

THE END TIMES

1. Coming World Events—1
   (Deut. 4:23-31;30:1-6)
2. Coming World Events—2
   (Ezek. 38-39)
3. Judgement of Christians
   (Rom. 14:10-21;1 Cor. 3:9-15;9:27;4:5;2 Cor. 5:10)
4. Seven-Year Tribulation
   (Deut. 4:30;Dan. 12:1;Matt. 24;Rev. 6-18)
5. Second Coming of Christ
   (Rev. 19:11-16)
6. The Millennium
   (Rev. 20:1-10)
7. Great White Throne Judgement
   (Rev. 20:11-15)
8. New Heaven and New Earth
   (Rev. 21-22)

Appendix 5

Training The Maturing Disciple

A. **Training Goal**
   To produce maturity and fruitfulness in the believer's life.
B. **Subject**
   Discipleship
C. **Number of Sessions**
   1. Lecture—8
   2. Home Share Group
      A. *Pathway to Discipleship*—36
      B. *Fishers of Men*—9
D. **Topics**
   1. What is a Disciple (2)
   2. How to Become a Disciple (1)
   3. Cost of Discipleship (1)
   4. Marks of a Disciple (2)
   5. How to Make Disciples (2)

E. Reference Materials
   1. Lecture
      Richard Booker, *Radical Christian Living* (Sounds of the Trumpet).
   2. Home Share Group
      A. *Pathway to Discipleship*—A series of four 9-week studies based upon the teachings of Jesus as set forth in the Beatitudes.
      B. *Fishers of Men*—A 9-week course teaching what the gospel is and how to present it.
F. Bible Study Outlines
   The following Bible Study Outlines are for the discipleship studies.

Study Outline Number 32

WHAT IS A DISCIPLE?

1. The Call to Discipleship
   (Matt. 28:18-20)
2. Aspects of Discipleship
   A. Follower
      (Matt. 4:18-22)
   B. Learner
      (Matt. 11:27-29;Rom. 12:1-2)
   C. Imitator
      (Eph. 5:1;Luke 6:40)
3. Results of Discipleship
   (Matt. 5:13-16)
   A. Salt
   B. Light

HOW TO BECOME A DISCIPLE

1. Self Death
   (John 6:38;Luke 9:23-24)
2. Dying to Live
   (Gal. 2:20;6:14)
3. Example of Communism
4. Letting Go of Self
   (John 12:24-25)
5. Contribution or Commitment?

Study Outline Number 34

THE COST OF DISCIPLESHIP

1. Counting the Cost
   (Luke 14:25-27)
2. Challenging the Crowd
   (Luke 14:28-33)
3. Prosperity Christian
   (Luke 9:57-58)
4. Self-Sufficient Christian
   (Luke 9:59-60)
5. Family Christian
   (Luke 9:61-62)

THE MARKS OF A DISCIPLE

1. Love
   (Eph. 5:1-2;John 13:34-35)
2. Fruit Bearing
   (John 15:1-8,16;Matt. 7:15-20)
3. Obedience
   (John 8:29-31;14:15,21;Luke 6:46;Matt. 7:21-27)
4. Submission
   (Matt. 26:39;11:28-30;28:18;Eph. 5:21)
5. Servanthood
   (John 13:13-17;Matt. 20:25-28;23:11-12;Luke 17:7-10)
6. Reproduction
   (John 12:23-25)

Study Outline Number 36

HOW TO MAKE DISCIPLES

1. Select
   (Luke 6:12-13;2 Tim. 2:2)
   A. Teachable Spirit—Ps. 139:23-24
   B. Hunger for God—Ps. 63:1-2
   C. Submitted to Lordship of Christ—Rom. 12:1-2
   D. Desire to be Used by God—Is. 6:8
   E. Concern for People—Phil. 1:8
2. Commit
   (Mark 3:14)
3. Teach
   (Acts 1:1)
4. Assign
   (Mark 6:7-13,30-32)
5. Send
   (John 20:21;Matt. 28:18-20)

Appendix 6

Training The Leader

A. **Training Goal**
   To develop the ability to lead others in spiritual growth and commitment.
B. **Subject**
   1. Helping Others
   2. Managing Your Life
C. **Number of Sessions**
   1. Lecture—8
   2. Home Share Group—9
D. **Topics**
   1. Helping Others (4)
   2. Managing Your Life (4)
E. **Reference Materials**
   1. Lecture
      A. J. Oswald Sanders, *Spiritual Leadership* (Moody Press).

B. Selwyn Hughes, *Helping People Through Their Problems* (Bethany House).
2. Home Share Group
Ministry Principles—A 9-lesson workbook designed for the purpose of teaching the essentials of effective ministry.
F. Bible Study Outlines
The following Bible Study Outlines are for the leadership studies.

Study Outline Number 37

HELPING OTHERS

1. Accept People as They are
(Rom. 15:7)
2. Listen Attentively
(James 1:19)
3. Show Genuine Concern and Compassion
(1 Pet. 3:8)
4. Evaluate the Area of Need
(1 Thess. 5:23)
   A. Physical
   B. Emotional
   C. Spiritual
5. Speak Positively to the Need
(Phil 4:8)
6. Maintain Confidences
(Prov. 11:13;20:19)

MANAGING YOUR LIFE

1. Establish Goals
   The goal is the long-term aim or purpose.
   (Prov. 29:18;Phil. 3:13-14)
2. Define Objectives
   The objectives are short-term milestones that tell you
   what you must do to meet your goal.
   (John 3:16)
3. Determine Priorities
   The priorities tell you when you want to accomplish your
   objectives
   (Rom. 1:16)
4. Develop Plans
   The plan tells you how you will accomplish your objec-
   tives.
   (Eph. 1:11;Gal. 4:4-5)

BIBLE STUDY MATERIALS BY RICHARD BOOKER

MINISTRY IN THE LOCAL CHURCH
Richard currently spends most of his time in a traveling ministry to the local church. If you are interested in having him come to your church, contact him directly at his Houston address.

CHRISTIAN GROWTH SEMINARS
Richard conducts a series of unique seminars in the local church. Each seminar is six hours long with a workbook in which the participant writes during the seminar. Current seminars are on prayer, personal Bible study, successful Christian living, and discipleship. Brochures are available from the ministry.

LOCAL CHURCH CENTERED BIBLE SCHOOLS
Richard has developed a Christian Growth Institute, which is a nine-month Bible school designed to be taught in the local church by the pastor or his associates. A catalog is available from the ministry.

BOOKS
Richard's books are superior quality teaching books. They uniquely communicate profound life-changing Bible truths with a rich depth, freshness and simplicity, and also explain how to apply what you have read to your life. His books are described on the following pages. You may order them through your bookstore or clip and mail the Book Order Form provided in the back of this book.

THE MIRACLE OF THE SCARLET THREAD
This book explains how the Old and New Testaments are woven together by the scarlet thread of the blood covenant to tell one complete story through the Bible.

COME AND DINE

This book takes the mystery and confusion out of the Bible. It provides background information on how we got the Bible, a survey of every book in the Bible and how each relates to Jesus Christ, practical principles, forms and guidelines for your own personal Bible study, and a systematic plan for effectively reading, studying and understanding the Bible for yourself.

WHAT EVERYONE NEEDS TO KNOW ABOUT GOD

This book is about the God of the Bible. It shows the ways in which God has revealed Himself to us and explains the attributes, plans and purposes of God. Then each attribute is related practically to the reader. This book takes you into the very heart of God and demonstrates how to draw near to Him.

RADICAL CHRISTIAN LIVING

This book explains how you can grow to become a mature Christian and help others do so as well. You'll learn the pathway to Christian maturity and how to select and train others in personal follow-up and discipling at different levels of Christian growth.

SEATED IN HEAVENLY PLACES

This book helps the reader learn how to live the victorious Christian life and walk in the power of God. It explains how to minister to others, wear the armor of God and exercise spiritual authority.

BLOW THE TRUMPET IN ZION

This book explains the dramatic story of God's covenant plan for Israel, including their past glory and suffering, their present crisis and their future hope.

JESUS IN THE FEASTS OF ISRAEL

This book is a study of the Old Testament feasts showing how they pointed to Jesus, as well as their personal and prophetic significance for today's world. The book points out how the Feasts represent seven steps to Christian growth and the peace, power and rest of God.

HOW TO PREPARE FOR THE COMING REVIVAL

There is a great expectancy in the hearts of believers everywhere that we are on the threshold of a great revival that will soon shake the world. This book explains the true meaning of revival and what we must do to prepare ourselves for a visitation from God.

AUDIO CASSETTE TAPE ALBUMS

A list of Richard's teaching cassettes is included on the following pages. All tape series come in an attractive album for your convenience. To order tapes, check the appropriate box, then clip and mail the Order Form which is provided on the last page of this book following the tape list.

BOOK ORDER FORM

Ordering Instructions
To order books, check the appropriate box, then clip and mail the coupon below to SOUNDS OF THE TRUMPET, INC., 8230 BIRCHGLENN, HOUSTON, TX 77070.

☐ Please send me _____ copy(ies) of THE MIRACLE OF THE SCARLET THREAD. I have enclosed $8.99 contribution for each copy ordered (price includes shipping).

☐ Please send me _____ copy(ies) of COME AND DINE. I have enclosed $8.99 contribution for each copy ordered (price includes shipping).

☐ Please send me _____ copy(ies) of WHAT EVERYONE NEEDS TO KNOW ABOUT GOD. I have enclosed $8.99 contribution for each copy ordered (price includes shipping).

☐ Please send me _____ copy(ies) of RADICAL CHRISTIAN LIVING. I have enclosed $8.99 contribution for each copy ordered (price includes shipping).

☐ Please send me _____ copy(ies) of SEATED IN HEAVENLY PLACES. I have enclosed $8.99 contribution for each copy ordered (price includes shipping).

☐ Please send me _____ copy(ies) of BLOW THE TRUMPET IN ZION. I have enclosed $8.99 contribution for each copy ordered (price includes shipping).

☐ Please send me _____ copy(ies) of JESUS IN THE FEASTS OF ISRAEL. I have enclosed $8.99 contribution for each copy ordered (price includes shipping).

☐ Please send me _____ copy(ies) of HOW TO PREPARE FOR THE COMING REVIVAL. I have enclosed $8.99 contribution for each copy ordered (price includes shipping).

☐ Please send me _____ copy(ies) of SUPERNATURAL PRAYER AND FASTING. I have enclosed $8.99 contribution for each copy ordered (price includes shipping).

☐ Please send me a free brochure describing your workshop on how to study the Bible.

☐ Foreign order please include an extra $2.00 for surface postage.

_____

Name _____

Street _____

City _____

State _____ Zip _____

TAPE ORDER FORM

Ordering Instructions

To order tapes, check the appropriate box, then clip and mail the coupon below to SOUNDS OF THE TRUMPET, INC., 8230 BIRCHGLENN, HOUSTON, TX 77070.

. . . .

☐ Please send me the following tapes. I have enclosed a $4.00 contribution for each tape ordered (No C.O.D.), plus $2.00 for mailing for each tape series.

☐ The Bible Series	($32.00)	☐ The Feasts Series	($24.00)
☐ Getting To Know God — 1	($16.00)	☐ The Sacrifices Series	($20.00)
☐ Getting To Know God — 2	($20.00)	☐ Love Notes from Jesus	($28.00)
☐ Getting To Know God — 3	($16.00)	☐ Ephesians Series	($48.00)
☐ Blood Covenant Series	($24.00)	☐ Philippians Series	($32.00)
☐ Abundant Life Series	($24.00)	☐ Colossians Series	($32.00)
☐ The Church Series	($24.00)	☐ Thessalonians Series	($32.00)
☐ The Christian Family	($16.00)	☐ Single Messages (Circle)	
☐ Faith & Healing Series	($12.00)	(SM 1, 2, 3, 4, 5, 6, 7	($4.00 each)
☐ End Times Series	($32.00)	8, 9, 10, 11, 12, 13	
☐ Prayer Series	($24.00)	14, 15, 16, 17, 18)	
☐ Foundational Studies — 1	($24.00)	☐ Practical Studies — 1	($24.00)
☐ Foundational Studies — 2	($24.00)	☐ Practical Studies — 2	($24.00)

Name _____

Street _____

City _____

State _____ ZIP_____

TAPE LIST

The Bible Series

BL1 Uniqueness of the Bible
BL2 How the Books Became the Book
BL3 Survey of Old Testament
BL4 Survey of New Testament
BL5 How We Got Our English Bible
BL6 Getting Into the Bible
BL7 How to Study the Bible
BL8 How to Understand the Bible

Getting to Know God — 1

KG1 Knowing God
KG2 The Self-Existing One
KG3 The Personal Spirit
KG4 The Trinity

Getting to Know God — 2

KG1 God Is Sovereign
KG2 God Is All Power
KG3 God Is All Knowledge
KG4 God Is Everywhere Present
KG5 God Never Changes

Getting to Know God — 3

KG1 God Is Holy
KG2 God Is Love
KG3 God Is Just
KG4 God Is Good

Blood Covenant Series

BC1 The Blood Covenant
BC2 What Was It Abraham Believed?
BC3 The Tabernacle
BC4 The Sacrifices
BC5 The High Priest
BC6 The Passover

Abundant Life Series

AL1 Knowing Your Dominion
AL2 Identify with Christ
AL3 Appropriating His Lordship
AL4 Walking in the Spirit
AL5 Ministering in the Spirit
AL6 Wearing the Armor

The Church Series

CH1 The Church
CH2 The Body of Christ
CH3 Gifts of the Spirit
CH4 Equipping the Saints
CH5 Work of the Ministry
CH6 Building Up the Body

Christian Family Series

CF1 God's Purpose for Family
CF2 The Husband's Role
CF3 The Wife's Role
CF4 Parent & Children Roles

Faith & Healing Series

FH1 Divine Healing Today
FH2 Basis for Claiming Healing
FH3 Barriers to Healing

End Time Series

ET1 Coming World Events — 1
ET2 Coming World Events — 2
ET3 Judgment of Christians
ET4 Seven-Year Tribulation
ET5 Second Coming of Christ
ET6 Millennium
ET7 Great White Throne Judgment
ET8 New Heaven & New Earth

The Feasts Series Tabernacles

FE1 Passover
FE2 Unleavened Bread
FE3 Pentecost
FE4 Trumpets
FE5 Atonement
FE6 Tabernacles

Sacrifices Series

SF1 Sin Offering
SF2 Trespass Offering
SF3 Burnt Offering
SF4 Meal Offering
SF5 Peace Offering